Contents

GUMDROP FRUITCAKE

INGREDIENTS

- 1 cup butter
- 2 cups white sugar
- 2 large eggs eggs, beaten
- 4 cups all-purpose flour
- 1 teaspoon ground cinnamon
- ¼ teaspoon ground cloves
- ¼ teaspoon ground nutmeg
- ¼ teaspoon salt
- 1 ½ cups applesauce
- 1 teaspoon baking soda
- 1 tablespoon hot water
- 1 teaspoon vanilla extract
- 16 ounces gumdrops, no black ones
- 3 cups raisins
- 1 cup chopped pecans
- 1 tablespoon butter

DIRECTIONS

Step 1

Preheat oven to 325 degrees F (165 degrees C). Line two 9 x 5 inch loaf pans or a 10 inch tube pan with greased parchment or heavy paper.

Step 2

Sift together the flour, cinnamon, cloves, nutmeg, and salt.

Step 3

Cut the gumdrops in fourths. Fry the pecans in the 1 tablespoon butter or margarine. Mix pecans, raisins, and gumdrops together, and roll in 3/4 cup of flour mixture.

Step 4

In a large bowl, cream together 1 cup butter or margarine and white sugar. Mix in beaten eggs. Mix in the flour and spice mixture alternately with the applesauce. Dissolve soda in hot water, and stir into batter. Stir in the vanilla. Stir in nuts, gumdrops, and raisins.

Step 5

Bake for 2 hours. The baking time for the tube pan should be about 30 to 40 minutes longer. Test about 10 minutes before the longer time. You may not get a clean tester, but you will be able to tell if it is the candy gumdrop or dough. Cool. Wrap in foil.

CRANBERRY PECAN CAKE

INGREDIENTS

- 3 cups frozen cranberries

- 1 cup pecans
- 1 cup white sugar
- 2 large eggs eggs
- 1 cup white sugar
- 1 cup all-purpose flour
- ½ cup butter, melted
- 2 tablespoons milk

DIRECTIONS

Step 1

Preheat oven to 350 degrees F (175 degrees C). Generously grease a 2 quart rectangular baking dish.

Step 2

Spread the cranberries evenly over the bottom of the baking dish, and sprinkle the pecans over the cranberries. Spoon 1 cup of sugar over the cranberries and pecans.

Step 3

Place the eggs into the work bowl of an electric mixer, and beat on high speed about 1 minute, until the eggs are foamy. Beat in 1 cup of sugar, the flour, melted butter, and milk, and beat on Low until just mixed. The batter will be thick. Spread the batter evenly over the cranberry-pecan mixture.

Step 4

Bake in the preheated oven until the cake is lightly brown and a toothpick inserted near the center comes out clean, 40 to 45 minutes. Carefully invert the cake onto a serving plate, so the cranberry-pecan layer is on top. Let cool 30 minutes before serving.

PECAN CHEESECAKE

INGREDIENTS

- 2 cups graham cracker crumbs
- ½ cup white sugar
- 1 teaspoon ground cinnamon
- ½ cup butter, melted
- 3 (8 ounce) packages cream cheese, softened
- 1 ¼ cups white sugar
- 3 large eggs eggs, room temperature
- ½ teaspoon vanilla extract
- ½ cup pecan liqueur
- 1 cup sour cream
- ¼ cup confectioners' sugar
- 1 teaspoon pecan liqueur
- 1 cup ground pecans
- ½ cup graham cracker crumbs
- 1 ½ tablespoons white sugar
- ½ teaspoon ground cinnamon
- ¾ cup pecan halves

DIRECTIONS

Step 1

Combine 2 cups graham cracker crumbs, 1/2 cup white sugar, 1 teaspoon cinnamon, and melted butter or margarine. Press firmly into the bottom of a 10 inch springform pan.

Step 2

In a large bowl, blend the cream cheese and 1 1/4 cup white sugar with an electric mixer at medium speed until well blended. Add the eggs, one at a time, blending well. Add vanilla extract. Add 1/2 cup liqueur, and blend for 5 minutes. Pour the filling on top of the crust

Step 3

Preheat the oven to 350 degrees F (175 degrees C). Bake for approximately 1 hour. The cake should be golden brown, and will have risen to the top of the pan. Turn off the heat, and let cool in the oven for 2 1/2 hours. When cool, remove the rim of the springform pan.

Step 4

In a small bowl, mix the sour cream, confectioners' sugar, and 1 teaspoon liqueur together. Spoon onto the top of the cooled cheesecake.

Step 5

In a small bowl, combine the finely ground pecans, finely ground graham cracker crumbs, 1 1/2 tablespoons white sugar, and cinnamon. Sprinkle the pecan topping on the cheesecake. Carefully press the pecan topping into the sides of the cheesecake. Garnish the top and sides with pecan halves.

SWEET FIGGY PUDDING

INGREDIENTS

- 1 cup all-purpose flour
- 1 cup soft bread crumbs
- 1 cup water
- 1 cup molasses
- 1 cup chopped dried figs
- 1 cup raisins
- ½ cup chopped walnuts
- ½ cup orange peel strips
- 1 teaspoon baking soda
- 1 teaspoon ground cinnamon
- 1 teaspoon ground cloves
- 1 teaspoon ground allspice
- 1 teaspoon ground nutmeg

DIRECTIONS

Step 1

Grease the inside bowl of a double-boiler.

Step 2

Mix flour, bread crumbs, water, molasses, figs, raisins, walnuts, orange peel, baking soda, cinnamon, cloves, allspice, and nutmeg together in a bowl until batter is well incorporated; spoon batter into the prepared double-boiler bowl and cover.

Step 3

Fill the bottom half of a double boiler with water and bring to a boil; reduce heat and simmer. Place bowl in the simmering water and cover. Steam until pudding is cooked through, adding water as needed, 3 hours. Cool slightly with cover ajar before serving warm.

MINI RED VELVET CUPCAKES WITH ITALIAN MERINGUE FROSTING

INGREDIENTS

- 1 ⅓ cups cake and pastry flour, sifted
- ⅔ cup granulated sugar
- 1 tablespoon unsweetened cocoa powder
- ½ teaspoon baking powder
- ¼ teaspoon baking soda
- ½ cup buttermilk
- ¼ cup butter, melted
- 1 egg
- 1 tablespoon red food colouring
- 1 teaspoon pure vanilla extract
- Edible gold flakes or sugar for garnish

Italian Meringue Frosting:

- ⅓ cup granulated sugar
- ¼ cup water
- 2 large egg whites egg whites
- Pinch cream of tartar
- ½ teaspoon pure vanilla extract

DIRECTIONS

Step 1

Preheat oven to 350 degrees F (175 degrees C). Grease 24 mini muffin cups or line with paper.

Step 2

In a large bowl, whisk together cake and pastry flour, sugar, cocoa powder, baking powder and baking soda; set aside.

Step 3

In another small bowl, whisk together buttermilk, melted butter, egg, food colouring and vanilla. Pour over flour mixture and whisk until smooth and well-combined. Divide batter among prepared muffin cups.

Step 4

Bake in the preheated oven for about 15 minutes or until toothpick in centre comes out clean. Remove from pan and let cool completely on rack.

Step 5

Italian Meringue Frosting: In a small saucepan, bring sugar and water to boil, stirring to dissolve sugar. Let mixture boil for 5 minutes.

Step 6

Meanwhile, in a large bowl, beat egg whites with cream of tartar until soft peaks form. While beating, add the hot sugar syrup in a steady stream and beat for about 5 minutes or until glossy stiff peaks form. Beat in vanilla.

Step 7

Frost the cupcakes and sprinkle with gold flakes or sugar as desired.

SANTA'S FAVORITE CAKE

INGREDIENTS

- 1 (18.25 ounce) package white cake mix
- 3 large egg whites egg whites
- 1 ⅓ cups buttermilk
- 2 tablespoons vegetable oil
- 1 (9 ounce) package yellow cake mix
- ½ cup buttermilk
- 1 egg
- 1 ½ tablespoons unsweetened cocoa powder
- 2 tablespoons red food coloring
- 1 teaspoon cider vinegar
- 1 (8 ounce) package cream cheese, softened
- 1 cup margarine, softened
- 2 (16 ounce) packages confectioners' sugar
- 2 teaspoons peppermint extract

DIRECTIONS

Step 1

Preheat oven to 350 degrees F (175 degrees C). Grease and flour three 9 inch round cake pans.

Step 2

In a large bowl, combine white cake mix, 3 egg whites, 1 1/3 cups buttermilk, and 2 tablespoons vegetable oil. Mix with an electric mixer for 2 minutes on high speed. In a separate bowl, combine yellow cake mix, 1/2 cup buttermilk, 1 egg, cocoa, red food coloring, and vinegar. Use an electric mixer to beat for 2 minutes on high speed.

Step 3

Spoon white batter alternately with red batter into the prepared cake pans. Swirl batter gently with a knife to create a marbled effect.

Step 4

Bake in preheated oven for 22 to 25 minutes, or until a wooden pick inserted into the centers comes out clean. Let cool in pans for at least 10 minutes before turning out onto a wire rack to cool completely.

Step 5

In a large bowl, beat cream cheese and margarine until smooth. Gradually blend in sugar until incorporated and smooth. Stir in peppermint extract. Spread peppermint cream cheese frosting between layers, and on top and sides of cake.

SNOW ON THE MOUNTAIN

INGREDIENTS

- 1 cup dates, pitted and chopped
- 1 cup chopped walnuts
- ½ cup all-purpose flour
- 1 cup white sugar
- 4 large eggs eggs
- 1 teaspoon baking powder
- ¼ teaspoon salt
- 2 teaspoons vanilla extract
- 5 fruit, without seeds oranges, peeled and cut into 5 or 6 pieces
- 3 medium (7" to 7-7/8" long)s bananas, cut into 1 inch pieces
- ¼ cup white sugar
- 1 pint heavy whipping cream
- ¼ cup confectioners' sugar
- 1 teaspoon vanilla extract

DIRECTIONS

Step 1

Preheat oven to 350 degrees F (175 degrees C). Grease and flour an 8 inch pan.

Step 2

In a medium bowl, beat together the eggs and 1 cup of sugar. Combine the flour, baking powder and salt, stir into the egg mixture. Then, stir in the dates, walnuts and vanilla. Pour into the prepared pan.

Step 3

Bake for 25 to 30 minutes in the preheated oven. Cool on the pan on a wire rack. When the cake is cooled, break into bite sized pieces. Stir the cake pieces together with the oranges, bananas and remaining sugar. Press into a medium sized bowl and chill for several hours.

Step 4

Invert cake onto a serving plate. Whip the heavy cream with the confectioners' sugar and vanilla until stiff. Spread over the entire cake.

DANISH RICE PUDDING WITH ALMONDS

INGREDIENTS

- 2 cups milk
- ⅓ cup Arborio rice
- ¼ cup chopped blanched almonds
- ¼ cup sherry
- ½ (.25 ounce) envelope unflavored gelatin
- ⅓ cup white sugar
- 1 teaspoon vanilla extract
- 1 cup heavy cream
- 1 (12 ounce) package frozen raspberries - thawed and drained

DIRECTIONS

Step 1

In a saucepan, bring the milk to a boil, and then add rice. Reduce heat to simmer, and continue cooking for 20 minutes, stirring occasionally. Remove from heat, and set aside to cool to room temperature.

Step 2

In a small saucepan, mix the sherry and gelatin; stir over low heat until the gelatin is dissolved. Stir in the sugar until completely dissolved, and then stir in vanilla. Stir into the rice with the chopped almonds. Refrigerate.

Step 3

Pour cream into a bowl, and whip until light and fluffy soft peaks appear. Fold into chilled rice pudding. Serve in small bowls, topped with frozen raspberries.

GINGERBREAD CHEESECAKE

INGREDIENTS

Cheesecake:

- aluminum foil
- 2 cups gingerbread cookie crumbs
- ¼ cup unsalted butter, melted
- 3 (8 ounce) packages cream cheese, at room temperature
- 1 cup dark brown sugar
- ⅓ cup unsulphured molasses
- 1 tablespoon lemon juice
- 1 tablespoon vanilla extract
- 2 teaspoons ground ginger
- 1 ½ teaspoons ground cinnamon
- ½ teaspoon ground cloves
- ½ teaspoon ground nutmeg
- ¼ teaspoon ground allspice
- 1 pinch salt
- 3 large eggs eggs, room temperature

Cinnamon Whipped Cream:

- 1 cup heavy whipping cream
- ¼ cup confectioners' sugar, or to taste
- ½ teaspoon vanilla extract
- ½ teaspoon cinnamon, or to taste
- 1 pinch salt

DIRECTIONS

Step 1

Preheat the oven to 350 degrees F (175 degrees C). Grease a 9-inch springform pan. Wrap the outside of the springform pan 3 to 4 times with aluminum foil.

Step 2

Mix cookie crumbs and melted butter together until mixture resembles wet sand. Press into the prepared springform pan until bottom is evenly covered.

Step 3

Combine cream cheese and brown sugar in a large bowl; beat with an electric mixer until smooth. Add molasses, lemon juice, vanilla extract, ginger, cinnamon, cloves, nutmeg, allspice, and salt; mix until well combined. Add eggs, 1 at a time, beating briefly after each addition until just combined. Pour batter over the crust in the pan. Tap the pan on the counter several times to remove any air bubbles.

Step 4

Place the springform pan into a larger baking pan, and fill the baking pan with 1 inch hot water, making sure no water gets into the cheesecake batter.

Step 5

Bake in the water bath in the preheated oven until the edges of the cheesecake are set and the middle jiggles slightly, about 1 hour. Turn off the oven without removing the cheesecake, leaving it inside until cooled, 1 to 2 hours.

Step 6

Remove from the oven and water bath. Run the tip of a table knife around the edges of the springform pan before removing to a serving platter. Refrigerate until completely chilled, at least 4 hours.

Step 7

Combine whipping cream, powdered sugar, vanilla extract, cinnamon, and salt for the cinnamon whipped cream in a large bowl. Beat with an electric mixer on medium-high speed until stiff peaks form; do not overmix.

Step 8

Top cheesecake with whipped cream just before serving.

SIMPLE CHRISTMAS RUM CAKE

INGREDIENTS

- cooking spray
- 1 (18.25 ounce) package yellow cake mix with pudding (such as Betty Crocker)
- 3 large eggs eggs

- ⅓ cup rum
- ½ cup water
- ½ cup vegetable oil
- ¼ cup rum
- ¼ cup water
- 1 cup white sugar
- ½ cup butter
- 1 teaspoon confectioners' sugar for sprinkling

DIRECTIONS

Step 1

Preheat oven to 350 degrees F (175 degrees C). Spray a fluted tube pan (such as a Bundt) with cooking spray.

Step 2

Place the cake mix, eggs, 1/3 cup of rum, 1/2 cup of water, and the vegetable oil into a large bowl. Beat until smooth with an electric mixer on low speed, about 3 minutes.

Step 3

Pour the batter into the prepared pan.

Step 4

Bake in the preheated oven until the cake has risen and the top is lightly golden brown, about 40 minutes. A toothpick inserted into the center of the cake should come out clean.

Step 5

While cake is baking, make the glaze. In a saucepan over medium heat, combine 1/4 cup of rum, 1/4 cup of water, sugar, and butter. Stir and heat until all the sugar has dissolved and the butter is melted. Turn off heat.

Step 6

Remove the cake from the oven. While still hot and in the pan, poke the cake all over with a long skewer to make many deep holes.

Step 7

Pour the glaze over the hot cake. Allow the cake to cool until the cake separates slightly from the side of the pan, 10 to 12 minutes.

Step 8

Line a jellyroll pan or large baking sheet with waxed paper. Carefully place the lined pan over the top of the cake pan, and flip the cake pan over to release the cake onto the waxed paper. If desired, transfer cake to a serving platter.

Step 9

Let the cake cool thoroughly and sprinkle lightly with confectioners' sugar before slicing.

CHOCOLATE-RASPBERRY

CHEESECAKE

INGREDIENTS

- 1 (150 g) package round shortbread cookies, finely crushed
- 1 tablespoon butter, melted
- 3 (250 g) packages PHILADELPHIA Chocolate Brick Cream Cheese, softened
- ¾ cup white sugar, divided
- 3 large eggs eggs
- 4 cups raspberries
- 1 tablespoon cornstarch
- 1 tablespoon water

DIRECTIONS

Step 1

Heat oven to 350 degrees F (175 degrees C).

Step 2

Mix cookie crumbs and butter; press onto bottom of 9-inch springform pan.

Step 3

Beat cream cheese and 1/2 cup sugar in large bowl with mixer until blended. Add eggs, 1 at a time, mixing on low speed after each just until blended; pour over crust.

Step 4

Bake 40 to 45 minutes or until centre is almost set. Run knife around rim of pan to loosen cake; cool before removing rim. Refrigerate cheesecake 4 hours.

Step 5

Meanwhile, cook raspberries and remaining sugar in saucepan on medium-high heat 12 to 14 minutes or until slightly thickened, stirring frequently. Mix cornstarch and water until blended. Add to raspberry mixture; cook and stir 1 minutes or until thickened. Pour through fine-mesh strainer into bowl; refrigerate until ready to serve.

Step 6

Serve cheesecake topped with raspberry sauce.

BLUE RIBBON WHIPPING CREAM POUND CAKE

INGREDIENTS

- 2 ½ cups white sugar
- 1 cup butter
- 7 large eggs eggs
- 6 tablespoons cornstarch
- 2 ⅝ cups all-purpose flour
- 1 cup heavy whipping cream

- 2 tablespoons vanilla extract

DIRECTIONS

Step 1

Preheat oven to 350 degrees F(175 degrees C). Grease and flour a 10 inch tube pan. Set aside.

Step 2

Cream together the sugar and butter until light. Continue beating and add 7 eggs, one at a time; beating well after each egg

Step 3

In a separate bowl, mix together flour and cornstarch. Beat half of the flour mixture into the egg and sugar mixture.

Step 4

Beat in 1/2 cup whipping cream, and then beat in the remainder of the flour mixture. Finish by beating in 1/2 cup more of whipping cream and vanilla.

Step 5

Pour into prepared pan and bake for about 60 to 75 minutes. Cool on rack for 10 minutes before turning it out onto a serving plate.

DELICIOUS WHOLE WHEAT FRUITCAKE COOKIES

INGREDIENTS

- 1 cup packed brown sugar
- 1 cup water
- 1 cup raisins
- 2 tablespoons butter
- ½ teaspoon salt
- 1 ½ cups whole wheat flour
- ¾ teaspoon baking soda
- ½ teaspoon ground ginger
- 1 teaspoon ground cinnamon
- ½ cup dates, pitted and chopped
- ½ cup candied mixed fruit peel, chopped
- ½ cup chopped nuts
- ½ cup chopped dried mixed fruit

DIRECTIONS

Step 1

Preheat oven to 350 degrees F (175 degrees C). Grease one 5x9 inch loaf pan.

Step 2

In a saucepan over medium heat, cook together the sugar, water, raisins, butter and salt. Remove from heat and allow to cool.

Step 3

Sift together the flour, soda, ginger and cinnamon. Stir into the cooled cooked mixture.

Step 4

Add the chopped dates, mixed peels, nuts and dried fruit.

Step 5

Pour into loaf pan and bake for 1 hour or drop by the teaspoon on a cookie sheet and bake for 15 minutes.

EASY EGGNOG POUND CAKE

INGREDIENTS

- 1 (18.25 ounce) package yellow cake mix
- ¾ cup butter, softened
- ¾ cup eggnog
- 1 (3.5 ounce) package instant vanilla pudding mix
- 4 large eggs eggs
- ½ teaspoon ground nutmeg
- 1 tablespoon confectioners' sugar, or as needed

DIRECTIONS

Step 1

Preheat oven to 350 degrees F (175 degrees C). Grease and flour a 10-inch fluted cake pan.

Step 2

Beat cake mix, butter, eggnog, and pudding mix together in a bowl with an electric mixer until just moistened. Add eggs and nutmeg; beat until batter is smooth, about 4 minutes. Pour batter into prepared cake pan.

Step 3

Bake in the preheated oven until a toothpick inserted in the center of the cake comes out clean, 40 to 45 minutes. Cool in the pan for 10 minutes before removing to a wire rack to cool completely. Dust with confectioners' sugar.

EGGNOG POUND CAKE

INGREDIENTS

- ¼ cup dried blueberries
- ¼ cup chopped dried cherries
- ¼ cup dried cranberries
- 2 tablespoons brandy
- 3 cups all-purpose flour
- 2 teaspoons baking powder
- ¼ teaspoon salt

- ⅛ teaspoon freshly grated nutmeg
- 1 cup unsalted butter, softened
- 2 cups white sugar
- 3 large eggs eggs
- 1 teaspoon vanilla extract
- 1 cup eggnog
- 2 tablespoons brandy
- 2 tablespoons water
- ¾ cup white sugar

DIRECTIONS

Step 1

In a small bowl, combine dried blueberries, dried cherries, dried cranberries, and 2 tablespoons brandy. Soak for 15 minutes.

Step 2

Preheat oven to 325 degrees F (165 degrees C). Grease and flour a 10 inch tube pan or Bundt pan. Sift together the flour, baking powder, salt, and nutmeg; set aside.

Step 3

In a large bowl, cream together the butter and 2 cups sugar until light and fluffy. Beat in the eggs one at a time, then stir in the vanilla. Beat in the flour mixture alternately with the eggnog, mixing just until incorporated. Fold in soaked fruit mixture. Spread batter into prepared pan.

Step 4

Bake in the preheated oven for 55 minutes, or until a toothpick inserted into the center of the cake comes out clean. Let cool in pan for 10 minutes, then turn out onto a wire rack.

Step 5

In a small bowl, mix together brandy, water, and 3/4 cup sugar. With pastry brush, brush entire surface of cake with glaze. Cool completely before serving.

PUMPKIN SPICE RING

INGREDIENTS

- 1 (18.25 ounce) package angel food cake mix
- 1 cup pumpkin puree
- ½ teaspoon pumpkin pie spice

DIRECTIONS

Step 1

Combine pumpkin and pumpkin pie spice, and mix well. Set aside.

Step 2

Mix cake as directed on package. Fold in pumpkin mixture. Pour into an ungreased tube pan.

Step 3

Bake at 350 degrees F (175 degrees C) until lightly browned, using the box directions as a guide to cooking time.

HOT MILK SPONGE CAKE

INGREDIENTS

- ¾ cup milk
- 2 tablespoons butter
- 3 large eggs eggs
- 1 ½ cups white sugar
- 1 ½ cups all-purpose flour
- 1 ½ teaspoons baking powder
- 1 teaspoon vanilla extract

DIRECTIONS

Step 1

Preheat oven to 350 degrees F (175 degrees C). Grease one large loaf pan or one 10 inch tube pan.

Step 2

In a saucepan over medium-low heat, combine the milk and the butter. Do not boil.

Step 3

In a large bowl beat the eggs until light colored. Gradually add the sugar to the eggs then stir in the flour and baking powder. Stir in the hot milk and butter. Beat only until combined. Stir in the vanilla. Pour the batter into the prepared pan.

Step 4

Bake at 350 degrees F (175 degrees C) for 45 to 50 minutes. Let cake cool in pan for 10 minutes. Remove cake from the pan and cool on a wire rack.

POOR MAN'S CAKE

INGREDIENTS

- 1 cup cold water
- 1 cup packed brown sugar
- 2 cups raisins
- ½ cup lard
- ½ teaspoon salt
- ½ teaspoon ground cinnamon
- ½ teaspoon ground nutmeg
- ¼ teaspoon ground cloves
- 1 ¾ cups all-purpose flour
- 1 teaspoon baking soda
- 1 teaspoon vanilla extract

DIRECTIONS

Step 1

Preheat oven to 350 degrees F (175 degrees C). Lightly grease one 9 x 13 inch pan.

Step 2

Place cold water, brown sugar, raisins, lard, salt, cinnamon, nutmeg, and cloves in a large saucepan. Bring this combination to a boil. Let simmer for a full 6 minutes, then allow mixture to cool to lukewarm. Set aside.

Step 3

In small mixing bowl, combine flour and soda. Gradually add the dry ingredients to the cooled mixture. Add vanilla, and blend into batter. Pour batter into prepared pan.

Step 4

Bake in the preheated oven for 90 to 120 minutes, or until a toothpick inserted into the center of the cake comes out clean. Allow to cool. Store for at least a week before cutting. This cake will remain moist for months.

GINGERBREAD POUND CAKE

INGREDIENTS

- 1 cup unsalted butter, softened
- 1 cup white sugar
- 5 large eggs
- 2 cups all-purpose flour
- 1 teaspoon ground ginger
- 1 teaspoon ground cinnamon
- 1 teaspoon ground cloves
- ½ teaspoon baking soda
- 1 cup molasses
- ½ cup sour cream
- Lemon Sauce (Optional):
- 1 cup water
- ½ cup white sugar
- 2 tablespoons cornstarch
- ⅓ cup lemon juice
- 1 tablespoon unsalted butter
- 2 teaspoons grated lemon zest
- ⅛ cup sifted powdered sugar, or to taste

DIRECTIONS

Step 1

Preheat the oven to 325 degrees F (165 degrees C). Grease and flour a 12-cup fluted tube pan (such as Bundt) well.

Step 2

Beat butter in a mixing bowl on medium speed until soft and creamy, about 2 minutes; gradually add 1 cup white sugar, beating at medium speed for 5 to 7 minutes. Add eggs one at a time, beating just until yellow disappears; batter may look a bit curdled.

Step 3

Combine flour, ginger, cinnamon, cloves, and baking soda in a separate bowl. Combine molasses and sour cream in another bowl. Add dry ingredients to the batter alternately with molasses mixture, beginning and ending with dry ingredients. Mix on low speed until each addition is just blended. Pour into the prepared pan.

Step 4

Bake in the preheated oven until a toothpick inserted into the center of the cake comes out clean, about 1 hour. Cool cake in the pan on a wire rack for 10 to 15 minutes; remove cake from pan and cool completely, about 30 minutes more.

Step 5

While cake cools, combine water, white sugar, and cornstarch in a saucepan; cook over medium heat, stirring constantly, until smooth and thickened. Stir in lemon juice, butter, and lemon zest and cook until warmed through.

Step 6

Sprinkle cooled cake with powdered sugar and serve with lemon sauce.

CHOCOLATE-PEPPERMINT CHEESECAKE

INGREDIENTS

- 1 ¼ cups chocolate cookie baking crumbs
- ¼ cup butter, melted
- 3 (250 g) packages PHILADELPHIA Chocolate Brick Cream Cheese, softened
- ¾ cup white sugar
- 1 teaspoon peppermint extract
- 3 large eggs eggs
- ½ cup whipping cream
- 1 tablespoon white sugar
- 1 candy cane, crushed

DIRECTIONS

Step 1

Heat oven to 350 degrees F (175 degrees C).

Step 2

Mix baking crumbs and butter; press onto bottom of 9-inch springform pan.

Step 3

Beat cream cheese and 3/4 cup sugar in large bowl with mixer until blended. Add extract; mix well. Add eggs, 1 at a time, mixing on low speed after each just until blended; pour over crust.

Step 4

Bake 40 to 45 minutes or until centre is almost set. Run knife around rim of pan to loosen cake; cool before removing rim. Refrigerate cheesecake 4 hours.

Step 5

Beat cream in separate bowl with mixer on high speed until soft peaks form. Gradually add remaining sugar, beating until stiff peaks form; spoon over cheesecake. Sprinkle with crushed candy.

CHESSCAKES

INGREDIENTS

- 1 (18.25 ounce) package white cake mix
- 2 (9 inch) unbaked pie crusts
- 1 (10 ounce) jar raspberry preserves

DIRECTIONS

Step 1

Preheat oven to 350 degrees F (175 degrees C). You will need two un-greased, 12-cup muffin tins for this recipe. (You may want to spray tops of muffin pans with nonstick cooking spray so cake does not stick).

Step 2

Prepare cake mix according to package directions; set aside. Roll out pastry dough to 18 inch thickness. Using a floured, round cookie cutter that is slightly bigger than the muffin cups, cut 24 circles of dough. Place one dough circle in each muffin cup, pressing dough gently into bottom and sides. Dough should come about halfway up the sides of each muffin cup.

Step 3

Place a rounded tablespoon of raspberry jam into each pastry-lined cup. Pour prepared cake batter into each cup over jam and pastry, filling just to the top of each cup.

Step 4

Bake in preheated oven for 25 to 30 minutes or until a toothpick inserted into the cake comes out clean. Let cool briefly in pans, then loosen with knife and remove cakes to wire rack to cool completely.

CHRISTMAS CRANBERRY CAKE WITH AMARETTO

INGREDIENTS

- 1 (15.25 ounce) package yellow cake mix
- 1 (3.4 ounce) package instant vanilla pudding mix
- 5 large eggs eggs
- ½ cup amaretto liqueur
- ½ cup vegetable oil
- ½ cup milk
- 2 cups chopped cranberries
- 1 cup flaked coconut
- 1 cup walnuts, chopped

Glaze:

- ¾ cup white sugar
- ½ cup amaretto liqueur
- 1 tablespoon butter

DIRECTIONS

Step 1

Preheat the oven to 350 degrees F (175 degrees C). Grease and flour a fluted tube pan (such as Bundt).

Step 2

Mix yellow cake mix, pudding mix, eggs, amaretto, oil, and milk together in a bowl. Beat using an electric mixer on medium speed for 2 to 3 minutes. Fold in cranberries, coconut, and walnuts. Pour into the prepared pan.

Step 3

Bake in the preheated oven until a toothpick inserted into the center comes out clean, about 55 minutes.

Step 4

Meanwhile, combine sugar, amaretto, and butter for glaze in a small saucepan. Bring to a boil; continue to boil until sugar is dissolved, 2 to 3 minutes.

Step 5

Remove cake from the oven and glaze immediately.

ANGEL FOOD ROLL WITH CRANBERRY FILLING

INGREDIENTS

- 1 ⅛ cups castor sugar or superfine sugar, divided
- ¾ cup sifted cake flour
- ¼ teaspoon salt
- 9 large egg whites egg whites
- 1 ½ teaspoons vanilla extract
- ¾ teaspoon cream of tartar
- ¼ cup confectioners' sugar for dusting
- 1 cup white sugar
- 2 ⅓ cups fresh or frozen cranberries
- 6 tablespoons water
- 2 tablespoons cornstarch
- ½ cup heavy cream
- 3 tablespoons confectioners' sugar

DIRECTIONS

Step 1

Preheat the oven to 300 degrees F (150 degrees C). Lightly grease a 10x15 inch jellyroll pan with cooking spray. Line with parchment paper.

Step 2

In a medium bowl, whisk together 1/2 cup of superfine sugar, cake flour and salt. Set aside. In a separate bowl, whip egg whites until foamy. Add vanilla and cream of tartar, and continue to whip. Gradually sprinkle in the remaining superfine sugar while continuing to whip the egg whites to firm peaks. Sift the flour mixture over the egg whites and fold in by hand using a rubber spatula. Spread the batter evenly in the prepared pan.

Step 3

Bake for 20 minutes in the preheated oven, or until the center of the cake springs back when lightly pressed. Cool in the pan over a wire rack. Generously sift sugar over the top of the cake, and cover with a clean towel. Run a spatula around the outside of the cake in the pan to loosen, and turn out onto the towel. Remove the parchment paper from the back of the cake, then place it back on loosely. Roll up with the towel loosely from short end to short end, and allow to cool in the rolled position.

Step 4

In a saucepan over medium heat, combine 1 cup of white sugar, cranberries and water. Simmer until the cranberries burst, about 5 minutes. Whisk in the cornstarch, and simmer just until thick, about 2 minutes. Transfer to a bowl, cover and refrigerate.

Step 5

Unroll the cake so that it is sitting flat on the towel. Spread the cooled cranberry filling over the top, leaving 1/2 inch border. Use the towel to help you keep a grip on the cake for an even roll. Roll up from short end to short end and place seam side down onto a platter. Refrigerate until serving.

Step 6

Whip cream with confectioners' sugar until soft peaks form. Serve slices of cake with a dollop of sweetened whipped cream.

NOEL FRUITCAKE

INGREDIENTS

- 3 ½ cups sifted all-purpose flour
- 1 ¼ teaspoons baking powder
- 1 teaspoon salt
- 2 teaspoons ground cinnamon
- ¼ teaspoon ground cloves
- 1 ¼ cups raisins
- 1 cup chopped pecans
- 12 ounces dried apricots, chopped
- 8 ounces candied cherries, halved
- 4 ounces candied lemon peel
- 4 ounces candied orange peel
- ½ cup orange juice
- 1 cup jellied cranberry sauce
- 1 ½ cups shortening

- 2 ½ cups packed light brown sugar
- 5 large eggs eggs
- 1 ½ cups chopped cranberries

DIRECTIONS

Step 1

Preheat oven to 300 degrees F (150 degrees C). Grease and flour a 10-inch tube pan. Line with parchment paper and grease the paper.

Step 2

In a medium bowl, sift flour, baking powder, salt, cinnamon and cloves together. Add raisins, pecans, apricots, cherries, lemon and orange peels. Toss to mix.

Step 3

In a small bowl, beat the orange juice and jellied cranberry sauce together until smooth. Set aside.

Step 4

In a large bowl, beat shortening, brown sugar and eggs together until fluffy. Add flour mixture alternately with the orange juice mixture, beginning and ending with the flour. Stir in the chopped cranberries just until the ingredients are well blended.

Step 5

Turn batter into the prepared pan. Bake for 3 1/2 to 4 hours or until the cake is golden brown. Cool cake in the pan. Remove from the pan and remove the paper. Store the cooled cake several weeks in a covered container to mellow flavors. You may also wrap the cake in a brandy-, whisky-, or rum-soaked cheesecloth before storing. If desired, garnish with orange slices and cranberries.

NO-BAKE CHOCOLATE YULE LOG WITH CHOCOLATE MUSHROOMS

INGREDIENTS

- 1 pint heavy cream
- 3 tablespoons unsweetened cocoa powder
- 5 tablespoons orange-flavored liqueur, such as Grand Marnier or Cointreau, divided
- 1 tablespoon sugar
- ¼ cup low-sugar orange marmalade
- 1 (9 ounce) box Nabisco Famous Chocolate Wafers
- 8 eaches nonpareils (or use chocolate stars or small Peppermint Patties)
- 8 eaches dark chocolate kisses, foil removed
- 1 (6 ounce) container raspberries

DIRECTIONS

Step 1

Beat cream, cocoa, 3 Tbs. liqueur and sugar to stiff peaks in a large bowl. Set aside. Mix marmalade with 2 Tbs. liqueur in a medium bowl. Select a platter long and wide enough to fit a 12-inch yule log with two 'knots.'

Step 2

On flat side of the first wafer, spread a scant teaspoon of marmalade and 1 1/2 tsps. of the cream mixture over entire surface, then top with another wafer, flat side up. Repeat until you have about 3 inches of wafers. Stand stack on its side at a slight angle on the serving platter. Keep adding to log until 16 wafers remain.

Step 3

Stack 8 wafers, also on a slight angle, on each side of the log to form two knots.

Step 4

Spread remaining whipped cream mix over whole log, coating completely, then create 'bark' by running fork tines along the log and each knot. Cover gently with plastic wrap and refrigerate at least 3 hours or overnight.

Step 5

Using a toothpick or ice pick, make a small hole in the bottom of each nonpareil. Stick a chocolate kiss into each hole to form mushrooms. Decorate log with clusters of mushrooms, and scatter raspberries around the platter. Slice and serve.

CRANBERRY CAKE ROLLS

INGREDIENTS

- PAM Baking Spray
- ½ cup confectioners' sugar, sifted
- 1 (15.25 ounce) package yellow cake mix
- 4 large eggs eggs
- ½ cup water
- 4 cups fresh or thawed frozen cranberries
- 1 ⅓ cups granulated sugar
- 1 ½ cups chopped pecans
- ½ cup orange marmalade, melted
- Reddi-wip Extra Creamy Whipped Cream

DIRECTIONS

Step 1

Preheat oven to 350 degrees F. Spray 2 (15x10x1-inch) baking pans with baking spray. Line with parchment paper; spray with additional baking spray. Set aside. Sprinkle 2 clean kitchen towels with 1/4 cup each confectioners' sugar; set aside.

Step 2

Beat cake mix, eggs and water in large bowl with electric mixer on low speed 30 seconds or until well blended. Beat on medium speed 2 minutes. Pour evenly into prepared pans.

Step 3

Bake 12 to 15 minutes or until wooden pick inserted in centers comes out clean. Run knife or small spatula around rims of pans to loosen cakes. Immediately invert each cake onto a prepared towel; remove pan. Carefully peel off paper. Starting at one of the short sides, roll up each cake and towel to form 2 separate rolls. Cool completely on wire racks.

Step 4

Meanwhile, combine cranberries and granulated sugar in medium saucepan; cook over medium heat 10 minutes or until juice of cranberries is released and sugar is dissolved, stirring occasionally. Stir in pecans. Cool completely.

Step 5

Unroll cakes. Spread 1/2 cup marmalade evenly over each cake to within 1 inch of edges; top evenly with cranberry mixture. Re-roll cakes, using towels as guide. Trim ends of each cake. Cut each cake into 10 slices. Top each slice with a serving of Reddi-wip. Serve immediately.

DARK GINGERBREAD WITH MAPLE WHIPPED CREAM

INGREDIENTS

Cake:

- 1 ½ cups all-purpose flour
- 1 teaspoon ground cinnamon
- ¾ teaspoon ground ginger
- ½ teaspoon baking soda
- ½ teaspoon baking powder
- ½ teaspoon salt
- ½ cup unsalted butter, softened
- ⅓ cup dark brown sugar, packed
- ⅓ cup dark corn syrup
- ⅓ cup molasses
- 1 egg
- ½ cup hot water
- ¼ cup chopped crystallized ginger
- Whipped Cream Topping:
- 1 cup heavy whipping cream, chilled
- 2 tablespoons pure maple syrup

DIRECTIONS

Step 1

Preheat oven to 350 degrees F (175 degrees C). Grease a 9-inch round or square pan and line bottom with parchment paper.

Step 2

Whisk flour, cinnamon, ground ginger, baking soda, baking powder, and salt together in a large bowl.

Step 3

Beat butter and brown sugar together in another large bowl with an electric mixer until light and fluffy, 3 to 4 minutes. Add corn syrup, molasses, and egg; beat until smooth. Pour in hot water slowly while continuing to beat. Add flour mixture gradually, mixing until batter is well-blended and smooth. Stir in crystallized ginger. Pour batter into the pan.

Step 4

Bake in the preheated oven until a toothpick inserted into the center comes out clean, 30 to 35 minutes. Cool in the pan, about 10 minutes. Run a knife around the edges and carefully invert onto a wire rack. Cut into wedges or squares.

Step 5

Whip heavy cream and maple syrup together in a large bowl until stiff peaks form. Serve whipped cream topping with cake.

GINGERBREAD CHEESECAKE BARS

INGREDIENTS

Cookie Base:

- 2 ¼ cups all-purpose flour
- 2 teaspoons ground ginger
- 1 teaspoon baking soda
- 1 teaspoon ground cinnamon
- ½ teaspoon ground cloves
- ¼ teaspoon salt
- ¾ cup margarine, softened
- 1 cup white sugar
- 1 egg
- ¼ cup molasses
- 1 tablespoon water

Filling:

- 2 (8 ounce) packages cream cheese
- ½ cup powdered sugar
- ½ cup brown sugar
- 6 tablespoons molasses
- 2 teaspoons ground ginger
- 2 teaspoons ground cinnamon
- ½ teaspoon ground nutmeg
- ½ teaspoon ground cloves
- 3 cups whipped topping
- 2 tablespoons whipped topping, or to taste

DIRECTIONS

Step 1

Preheat the oven to 350 degrees F (175 degrees C).

Step 2

Sift together flour, ginger, baking soda, cinnamon, cloves, and salt for the cookie base in a bowl.

Step 3

Cream margarine and white sugar in a large bowl with an electric mixer until light and fluffy. Add egg and beat until well combined. Stir in molasses and water. Gradually stir flour mixture into the molasses mixture. Transfer dough to a 9x13-inch pan, patting it down so it covers the entire bottom of the pan.

Step 4

Bake in the preheated oven until lightly browned, 25 to 30 minutes. Allow to cool completely.

Step 5

Beat cream cheese, powdered sugar, and brown sugar for the filling in a large bowl with an electric mixer until smooth. Add molasses, ginger, cinnamon, nutmeg, and cloves and stir, scraping down the sides of the bowl, until mixture is smooth. Fold in 3 cups whipped topping until well combined. Spread filling into the cooled cookie base. Cover with plastic wrap and refrigerate until set, at least 4 hours or overnight.

Step 6

Garnish with remaining whipped topping before serving.

SAFFRON AND COINTREAU CHEESECAKE ON GINGERBREAD

INGREDIENTS

- 1 (8 ounce) package ginger nut cookies (biscuits)
- ½ cup butter, melted
- ¼ cup Cointreau or other orange liqueur
- ½ (.5 gram) packet saffron threads
- 5 (3 ounce) packages cream cheese
- ½ cup honey
- 1 ½ tablespoons finely-grated orange zest
- 1 ¾ cups heavy cream

DIRECTIONS

Step 1

Place the cookies and butter in a blender. Blend until you have a slightly-moist and crumbly mixture. Press the crumbs into the base of a 9 inch springform pan; refrigerate.

Step 2

Heat the Cointreau in a small saucepan until it begins to steam; add the saffron threads. Remove from heat and allow to rest for 20 minutes.

Step 3

Beat the cream cheese with an electric hand mixer on low speed until softened. Slowly beat in the honey and orange zest. Add the saffron mixture and continue to beat. Pour in the cream while continuing to beat on the lowest speed until the mixture is thick enough to firmly hold its shape. Spoon the mixture over the crust. Chill overnight.

EASY CRANBERRY CHEESECAKE

INGREDIENTS

- ¾ cup graham cracker crumbs
- ½ cup chopped macadamia nuts
- ¼ cup melted margarine
- 2 tablespoons white sugar
- ¼ cup cold water
- 1 (.25 ounce) envelope unflavored gelatin
- 2 (8 ounce) packages cream cheese, softened
- 1 (7 ounce) jar marshmallow creme
- 1 (16 ounce) can whole berry cranberry sauce
- 1 cup frozen whipped topping (such as Cool Whip), thawed

DIRECTIONS

Step 1

Preheat oven to 350 degrees F (175 degrees C).

Step 2

Mix graham cracker crumbs, macadamia nuts, margarine, and sugar together in a bowl; press into the bottom of a 9-inch springform pan.

Step 3

Bake in the preheated oven until crust is lightly browned, about 10 minutes. Cool crust.

Step 4

Mix water and gelatin together in a saucepan over low heat until dissolved, 3 to 4 minutes.

Step 5

Beat cream cheese and marshmallow cream together in a bowl using an electric mixer on medium speed until well mixed. Gradually stir gelatin mixture and cranberry sauce into cream cheese mixture; fold in whipped topping. Spoon mixture over crust. Chill cheesecake in the refrigerator until firm, at least 1 hour.

CHURRO LOG CABIN

INGREDIENTS

- 1 (16 ounce) package canned white frosting
- 16 eaches pre-made churros (such as Tio Pepe's)
- 1 box toothpicks
- 7 cracker (2-1/2" square)s graham crackers
- 1 (14 ounce) package red licorice
- 1 cup gumdrops
- 1 cup small (2 1/2 inch tall) peppermint candy canes

- 1 (1.75 ounce) package holiday sprinkles
- 1 cup peppermint candies
- 2 cups shredded coconut
- ¼ cup confectioners' sugar

DIRECTIONS

Step 1

Cabin Base: Fill a piping bag with frosting. Pipe a line of frosting along one side of a churro; lay frosting-side down on a serving platter. Repeat with 3 additional churros to form a square. Repeat with a second layer of churros, stacking them frosting side down on top of base layer. Repeat until walls are 4 churros high. Stick toothpicks vertically through churros at each corner for structural stability.

Step 2

Roof: Center a graham cracker across the top of the cabin, using frosting to adhere it to the tops of the cabin walls. Lay a second graham cracker next to it; it will overhang the side of the cabin a bit. Adhere it with frosting. Repeat with a third graham cracker on the other side. Measure and cut 2 pieces of red licorice to the same length as the graham crackers, about 4x 3/4 inches; glue with frosting down the center of the middle graham cracker about 3 inches apart. These will hold up the A-frame roof. To form the A- frame, frost the long sides of 2 graham crackers and lean them together so top long sides meet and bottom long sides are set just inside the licorice lines. Decorate roof with licorice and gumdrops as desired.

Step 3

Cabin Door: Break a graham cracker in half widthwise, spread a thin layer of frosting on one side, then decorate with candy canes and holiday sprinkles. Frost backside of door and stick it to the front of the log cabin.

Step 4

Windows: Break a graham cracker into quarters. Spread 3 quarters with a thin layer of frosting and decorate as desired. Frost backside of windows and stick them to sides and back of cabin.

Step 5

Icicles and Snow: Pipe frosting icicles along roofline, sprinkle coconut around cabin, and sift confectioners' sugar over the top.

CRANBERRY SWEET POTATO SPICE CAKE

INGREDIENTS

- 3 cups all-purpose flour
- 2 teaspoons baking soda
- 2 teaspoons baking powder
- 2 teaspoons ground cinnamon
- 2 teaspoons ground nutmeg
- ½ teaspoon salt
- 1 ½ cups butter

- 1 ½ cups white sugar
- 3 large eggs eggs
- ½ cup molasses
- 1 tablespoon vanilla extract
- 3 cups cooked mashed sweet potatoes
- 1 ½ cups sweetened dried cranberries (such as Craisins)
- 1 cup chopped walnuts

DIRECTIONS

Step 1

Preheat oven to 350 degrees F (175 degrees C). Grease and flour two 9-inch round baking pans.

Step 2

Sift flour, baking soda, baking powder, cinnamon, nutmeg, and salt together in a bowl.

Step 3

Beat butter and sugar together in a separate large bowl with an electric mixer until light and fluffy. Beat one egg at a time into the butter mixture; add molasses and vanilla extract with last egg. Add sweet potatoes, cranberries, and walnuts; mix until batter is thoroughly combined. Gradually beat flour mixture into batter until thoroughly combined. Pour batter into prepared baking pans.

Step 4

Bake in preheated oven until a toothpick inserted into the center comes out clean, about 1 hour 10 minutes. Cool in the pans for 10 minutes before turning out onto wire rack to cool completely.

LOVING LOAF

INGREDIENTS

- ½ cup melted butter
- ⅓ cup white sugar
- 1 ½ cups crushed vanilla wafers
- 1 cup chopped pecans
- 1 cup butter, softened
- 2 cups white sugar
- 4 large eggs eggs
- 1 cup milk
- 2 teaspoons vanilla extract
- 2 ⅔ cups all-purpose flour
- 1 ½ teaspoons baking powder
- 1 teaspoon salt

DIRECTIONS

Step 1

Preheat oven to 350 degrees F (175 degrees C). Grease two 8x4 inch bread pans.

Step 2

Prepare the topping by combining the 1/2 cup butter, 1/3 cup sugar, vanilla wafers and pecans. Mix together well and press into the bottom of prepared pans.

Step 3

Cream butter and sugar together. Add eggs one at a time and beat well. Combine milk and vanilla.

Step 4

Sift flour, baking powder, and salt. Add to batter, alternating with milk; beat well. Pour into prepared loaf pans.

Step 5

Bake in preheated oven at 350 degrees F (175 degrees C) for 1 hour, or until a toothpick inserted into the cake comes out clean. Remove from oven and cool on wire rack.

FROZEN CHRISTMAS PUDDING

Servings: 8 **Yield:** 8 servings

INGREDIENTS

- ½ cup raisins
- ½ cup sultana raisins
- ½ cup dried currants
- ¼ cup candied cherries, chopped
- ¼ cup candied mixed fruit peel
- ¼ cup fruit juice
- ¼ cup almonds
- 1 teaspoon ground cinnamon
- 1 teaspoon freshly grated nutmeg
- ½ cup heavy whipping cream
- 4 ¼ cups chocolate ice cream, softened

DIRECTIONS

Step 1

In a medium bowl, combine fruit with fruit juice and spices. Cover, and allow to stand overnight.

Step 2

The next day mix together soaked fruits, almonds, cream, and ice cream. Pour mixture into a large mold, and cover with foil. Freeze for at least one week to allow flavour to develop.

Step 3

Unmold by quickly dipping into hot water, and inverting onto serving plate.

ALMOND POUND CAKE

INGREDIENTS

- 1 cup butter, softened
- 2 cups white sugar
- 6 large eggs eggs, room temperature

- 1 ¾ cups all-purpose flour
- ½ teaspoon salt
- 2 teaspoons almond extract
- 8 ounces almond paste
- 1 cup confectioners' sugar
- 4 tablespoons milk
- ½ cup blanched almonds
- 4 drops red food coloring
- 4 drops green food coloring

DIRECTIONS

Step 1

Preheat oven to 325 degrees F (165 degrees C). Grease and flour a 10 inch Bundt pan.

Step 2

In a large bowl, cream butter and sugar together until well mixed with an electric mixer. Add eggs, one at a time, and beat until mixture is light and fluffy. Blend in flour and salt. Mix in almond extract. Turn batter into prepared pan.

Step 3

Bake for 60 minutes, or until a toothpick when inserted in the center of the cake comes out clean. Cool in pan for 10 minutes. Remove from pan, and transfer to a wire rack to continue cooling.

Step 4

Break off tablespoon-sized pieces of the almond paste, and shape into holly leaves. Using the tip of a knife, score the shaped holly leaf to resemble veins in the leaves. Mix green food coloring with a small amount of water and brush the holly leaves, repeating until desired color is reached. Set aside on waxed paper. Break off 2 tablespoons of almond paste, and knead in several drops of red food coloring. When color of almond paste is a bright red, break off smaller pieces. Roll into balls to resemble holly berries. Place on waxed paper.

Step 5

In a small bowl, combine 1 cup confectioners' sugar and milk. Mix until smooth. When the cake has cooled, drizzle with the confectioners' sugar glaze. Top with blanched almonds, and garnish with the marzipan holly leaves and berries.

BEER SPICE CAKE

INGREDIENTS

- 1 ½ cups all-purpose flour
- 1 teaspoon baking powder
- 1 teaspoon ground cloves
- 1 teaspoon ground cinnamon
- 1 teaspoon ground allspice
- ½ teaspoon baking soda
- ¼ teaspoon salt
- ½ cup butter or margarine, softened

- 1 cup brown sugar
- 1 egg, beaten
- 1 cup beer
- 1 cup chopped walnuts

DIRECTIONS

Step 1

Preheat oven to 375 degrees F (190 degrees C). Grease and flour a 9x5 inch loaf pan.

Step 2

Sift together flour, baking powder, cloves, cinnamon, allspice, baking soda, and salt in a bowl. Set aside.

Step 3

In a large bowl, cream the butter and brown sugar until light and fluffy. Add egg and beat well. Add flour mixture alternately with beer and mix well to combine. Fold in the chopped walnuts.

Step 4

Pour into a 9x5 inch loaf pan. Bake 40 to 50 minutes in the preheated oven, or until a toothpick inserted into the cake comes out clean.

ICELANDIC CHRISTMAS CAKE

INGREDIENTS

- 1 cup white sugar
- ¾ cup butter
- 2 large eggs eggs
- 2 ½ cups all-purpose flour
- 2 teaspoons baking powder
- ¾ cup milk
- ½ cup raisins
- ½ teaspoon lemon extract
- ½ teaspoon cardamom flavored extract

DIRECTIONS

Step 1

Preheat oven to 350 degrees F (175 degrees C). Grease one 11 inch loaf pan.

Step 2

Cream the butter or margarine and the sugar until light and fluffy. Add the eggs one at time beating well after each one. Stir in the milk, lemon and cardamom flavorings. Stir in the flour and the baking powder.

Step 3

Sift a little flour over the raisins then stir them into the batter. Pour the batter into the prepared pan.

Step 4

Bake at 350 degrees F (175 degrees C) for 55 to 60 minutes.

CHOCOLATE PLUM PUDDING CAKE

INGREDIENTS

- ⅔ cup raisins
- ¾ cup all-purpose flour
- ¾ cup whole wheat flour
- ⅓ cup unsweetened cocoa powder
- 2 teaspoons baking soda
- ¼ teaspoon salt
- 1 tablespoon ground cinnamon
- ½ teaspoon ground nutmeg
- ¾ cup butter, softened
- 1 ½ cups white sugar
- 3 large eggs eggs
- 2 cups applesauce
- ½ cup coarsely chopped walnuts

DIRECTIONS

Step 1

Preheat oven to 350 degrees F (175 degrees C). Place raisins in a small saucepan, and cover with boiling water. Soak for 5 minutes, then drain. Grease and flour a 9 inch tube pan.

Step 2

Sift together the all-purpose flour, whole wheat flour, cocoa, baking soda, salt, cinnamon, and nutmeg. Set aside.

Step 3

In a large bowl, cream butter and sugar until light and fluffy. Blend in the eggs, then the applesauce. Beat in the flour mixture. Stir in raisins and walnuts. Spread batter evenly into prepared tube pan.

Step 4

Bake in preheated oven for 80 minutes, or until a toothpick inserted in the center of cake comes out clean. Let cool in pan for 10 minutes, then turn out onto a wire rack and cool completely; chill.

DEEP DARK CHOCOLATE PEPPERMINT CAKE

INGREDIENTS

- 2 cups sifted cake flour
- ¾ teaspoon salt
- 4 (1 ounce) squares unsweetened chocolate
- ¼ cup butter
- 2 cups white sugar
- 2 large egg yolks egg yolks
- 1 ¾ cups milk, divided

- 1 teaspoon vanilla extract
- 1 teaspoon baking soda
- Seven-Minute Frosting
- ½ cup crushed peppermint hard candies
- 3 drops red food coloring

DIRECTIONS

Step 1

Preheat oven to 350 degrees F (175 degrees C). Grease two 9-inch round pans and line the bottoms with parchment paper.

Step 2

Sift together the cake flour and salt.

Step 3

Melt chocolate and butter together in a double boiler. Turn into mixing bowl, and cool to room temperature; this mixture must be cool. Mix in the sugar. Blend in egg yolks and 1 cup milk.

Step 4

Pour in the flour and salt, and mix just until incorporated. Beat batter with electric mixer for 1 minute, and then blend in vanilla and 1/2 cup milk. Dissolve baking soda in the remaining 1/4 cup milk; stir into the batter quickly and thoroughly. Pour batter into prepared pans.

Step 5

Bake in the preheated oven until the surface of the cakes spring back lightly when pressed with a finger, about 30 minutes. Cool cakes on wire racks.

Step 6

Prepare Seven Minute Frosting, omitting vanilla (see Footnote for link). Tint the frosting a delicate pink with a few drops of food coloring, and add 1/4 cup crushed candy. Frost and fill the cooled cake. Garnish with bits of crushed candy.

PLUM PUDDING

INGREDIENTS

- ½ cup butter, room temperature
- 1 cup white sugar
- 6 large eggs eggs, room temperature
- ½ cup chopped candied citron
- 1 ½ cups pitted prunes, chopped
- ½ cup raisins
- 1 cup coarsely chopped pecans
- ½ cup all-purpose flour
- 1 ½ cups fine dry bread crumbs
- 1 teaspoon ground cinnamon
- 1 teaspoon ground nutmeg
- ½ teaspoon ground allspice

DIRECTIONS

Step 1

Preheat oven to 350 degrees F (175 degrees C). Grease and flour a 2 quart souffle or casserole dish.

Step 2

In a large bowl, cream together the butter and sugar until light and fluffy. Beat in the eggs one at a time.

Step 3

In a separate bowl combine the citron, prunes, raisins and pecans. Stir in the flour and toss so that everything is coated with flour.

Step 4

To the butter mixture add the fruit and nut mixture along with the bread crumbs, cinnamon, nutmeg and allspice. Mix well and transfer to prepared dish.

Step 5

Bake in preheated oven for 50 to 55 minutes, or until well browned.

CRANBERRY PUDDING

INGREDIENTS

- 2 cups cranberries
- 1 ½ cups all-purpose flour
- ½ teaspoon salt
- ½ teaspoon baking soda
- ⅓ cup boiling water
- ½ cup molasses
- 1 cup white sugar
- ½ cup butter, softened
- ½ cup heavy whipping cream
- 1 teaspoon vanilla extract

DIRECTIONS

Step 1

Lightly grease a 2-quart metal pudding mold or a clean 1-pound coffee can. Pick over whole cranberries; wash and drain.

Step 2

Sift together the flour and salt; dredge cranberries in flour mixture.

Step 3

Dissolve soda into boiling water and add molasses. Stir and allow to foam up.

Step 4

Add to the flour and cranberry mixture. Mix together until well blended. Spoon into prepared mold or pan; cover with a double layer of aluminum foil and fasten with heavy elastic band or string.

Step 5

Place into a deep saucepan and fill with water up to about the halfway mark on the pudding can. Cover saucepan and place over high heat. Bring water to boil, reduce heat, and simmer for 1 hour. Remove from water and allow to cool.

Step 6

Prepare the sauce by mixing together the sugar, butter and cream. Cook over medium heat until thick, stirring constantly. Remove from heat and add vanilla.

Step 7

When ready to serve the pudding, invert pan or open bottom of can and push through. Slice in 1/2-inch pieces. Pour sauce over individual slices of pudding.

EGGNOG CHEESECAKE

INGREDIENTS

- 1 cup graham cracker crumbs
- 3 tablespoons white sugar
- 3 tablespoons butter, melted
- 4 (8 ounce) packages cream cheese, softened
- 1 cup white sugar
- 3 tablespoons all-purpose flour
- 4 large eggs eggs
- 1 cup eggnog
- 1 teaspoon vanilla extract

DIRECTIONS

Step 1

Lightly grease a 9-inch springform pan. Combine the graham cracker crumbs, 3 tablespoons white sugar, and butter in a bowl and mix until evenly moistened; press into the bottom of the prepared pan.

Step 2

Cream together the cream cheese and 1 cup sugar using an electric mixer. Add the flour and beat until smooth. Mix in the eggs with the mixer switched to low. Pour in the eggnog and vanilla; continue beating until just blended. Stop the mixer and scrape the bottom of the bowl occasionally. Pour the mixture over the crust.

Step 3

Fill a shallow dish with some hot water and place on bottom rack of the oven. Put cheesecake on the middle rack of the oven. Turn oven heat to 200 degrees F (95 degrees C). Do not preheat oven.

Step 4

Bake the cheesecake until the center is set, about 3 hours 15 minutes. Turn oven off. Allow cheesecake to cool in the oven, about 3 hours. Chill in refrigerator overnight.

CHOCOLATE BAR TORTE

INGREDIENTS

- 1 cup milk
- 2 tablespoons milk
- 48 regulars large marshmallows, chopped
- 8 (1.55 ounce) bars chocolate candy (such as Hershey's)
- 3 cups heavy whipping cream
- 30 large rectangular piece or 2 squares or 4 small rectangular pieces graham cracker squares, crushed
- ¼ cup white sugar
- 6 tablespoons butter, melted

DIRECTIONS

Step 1

Pour both amounts of milk into a saucepan, place over medium heat, and bring milk almost to a simmer, stirring often. Add marshmallows and chocolate candy bars. Stir until marshmallows and chocolate melt and the mixture is smooth. Set aside to cool.

Step 2

Whip cream in a large bowl until fluffy and cream holds stiff peaks when beaters are lifted straight up, about 5 minutes. Gently fold cooled marshmallow mixture into whipped cream.

Step 3

Combine graham cracker crumbs, sugar, and butter until crust mixture is evenly moist. Press mixture into the bottom of a 9x13-inch dish. Spread marshmallow filling evenly over the crumb crust. Refrigerate until set, about 2 hours.

EXCELLENT APPLE GINGERBREAD

INGREDIENTS

- ¼ cup butter
- 3 eaches Granny Smith apples - peeled, cored and chopped
- ¾ cup butter at room temperature
- 1 tablespoon honey
- ½ cup white sugar
- ½ cup packed brown sugar
- 2 large eggs eggs
- 2 cups all-purpose flour
- 2 teaspoons baking soda
- 2 teaspoons ground cinnamon
- 1 teaspoon pumpkin pie spice
- 1 teaspoon ground cloves
- ½ teaspoon ground ginger
- ¼ teaspoon salt
- ½ cup milk
- ½ cup chopped walnuts
- 1 egg white
- 1 teaspoon ground cinnamon

- ½ cup chopped walnuts
- 1 tablespoon brown sugar
- ½ cup butter, softened
- 1 cup confectioners' sugar
- 1 (8 ounce) package cream cheese, softened
- 1 teaspoon vanilla extract
- 1 (20 ounce) can apple pie filling

DIRECTIONS

Step 1

Melt 1/4 cup of butter in a large skillet over medium heat. Add the apples; cook and stir until tender. Set aside and allow to cool.

Step 2

Preheat the oven to 350 degrees F (175 degrees C). Grease and flour two 9 inch round cake pans.

Step 3

In a large bowl, mix 3/4 cup of butter, honey, brown sugar and white sugar until light and fluffy using an electric mixer. Beat in the eggs one at a time, mixing each one until blended. Combine the flour, baking soda, cinnamon, pumpkin pie spice, cloves, ginger and salt; stir into the batter, alternating with the milk. Stir in the walnuts and cooked apples just until evenly distributed. Divide evenly between the prepared pans and spread evenly.

Step 4

Bake the cake in the preheated oven until a toothpick inserted in the center comes out clean, about 30 minutes. Cool the cakes on a wire rack. Keep the oven on for the walnuts.

Step 5

To make the candied walnuts for the top of the cake, whip the egg whites in a clean bowl until foamy. Stir in the brown sugar, cinnamon and walnuts. Spread the nuts out on a baking sheet.

Step 6

Bake in the preheated oven until toasted and fragrant, about 10 minutes. Cool completely before using.

Step 7

To make the frosting, mix together the butter, confectioners' sugar and cream cheese until smooth. Place one layer of cake on a serving plate and spread with a thin layer of the cream cheese icing. Top with most of the apple filling and spread evenly. Place the other layer of cake on top with the bottom facing up. Spread remaining cream cheese icing over the top and sides. Decorate the top with remaining apple filling and sprinkle with candied walnuts.

FRUIT CAKE

INGREDIENTS

- 1 serving cooking spray with flour
- 1 (18.25 ounce) package lemon cake mix (such as Duncan Hines Lemon Supreme)
- 4 large eggs eggs

- ½ cup vegetable oil
- 1 (3 ounce) package instant lemon pudding mix
- 1 tablespoon lemon extract
- 1 tablespoon vanilla extract
- 8 ounces candied red cherries, halved
- 8 ounces candied pineapple slices, cut into thirds
- 1 ½ cups chopped pecans
- 1 cup sweetened dried cranberries

DIRECTIONS

Step 1

Preheat oven to 325 degrees F (165 degrees C). Spray a 9-inch fluted tube pan, such as a Bundt, with cooking spray.

Step 2

Mix the cake mix, eggs, vegetable oil, lemon pudding mix, lemon extract, and vanilla extract together in a large bowl until smooth, and stir in candied cherries, pineapple, pecans, and dried cranberries. Pour the batter into the prepared cake pan.

Step 3

Bake in the preheated oven until a toothpick inserted into the center of the cake comes out clean, about 1 hour and 15 minutes. Allow to cool in the pan for 20 minutes before turning it out onto a cake plate to finish cooling. Store in a covered container to help retain moisture.

FLUFFY PUMPKIN SPICED CUPCAKES

INGREDIENTS

- 1 (15 ounce) can pumpkin puree
- 1 ½ cups white sugar
- 1 cup packed brown sugar
- ½ cup butter-flavored shortening
- ½ cup butter, softened
- ¼ cup whole milk
- ¼ cup vegetable oil
- 4 large eggs eggs
- 2 cups cake flour
- ¼ cup dry buttermilk powder
- ¼ cup cornstarch
- 2 teaspoons pumpkin pie spice
- 2 teaspoons baking powder
- 1 teaspoon baking soda
- ¾ teaspoon salt

DIRECTIONS

Step 1

Preheat oven to 350 degrees F (175 degrees C). Line 24 muffin cups with paper muffin liners.

Step 2

Beat the pumpkin puree, white sugar, brown sugar, shortening, butter, milk, vegetable oil, and eggs together in a large bowl until smooth. Whisk the cake flour, dry buttermilk powder, cornstarch, pumpkin pie spice, baking powder, baking soda, and salt together in another bowl. Add the dry ingredients to the pumpkin mixture, stirring until mixed. Pour batter into the prepared muffin cups, filling each cup about 2/3 full.

Step 3

Bake in the preheated until the center of the cupcakes spring back when touched, about 30 minutes. Cool in the pans for 10 minutes before removing to cool completely on a wire rack.

FLOURLESS CHOCOLATE ESPRESSO CAKE

INGREDIENTS

Cake:

- 1 tablespoon instant espresso powder
- 1 tablespoon hot water
- ¾ cup LAND O LAKES Unsalted Butter
- 6 ounces high-quality bittersweet chocolate baking bar, broken into small pieces
- 1 cup sugar
- 3 eaches LAND O LAKES Eggs
- ½ cup unsweetened cocoa powder

Espresso Whipped Cream:

- 1 teaspoon instant espresso powder
- 1 teaspoon hot water
- 1 cup LAND O LAKES Heavy Whipping Cream, chilled
- ¼ cup sugar
- 2 tablespoons powdered sugar
- ⅛ teaspoon extra fine edible glitter

DIRECTIONS

Step 1

Heat oven to 350 degrees F.

Step 2

Wrap outside of 9-inch springform pan with aluminum foil. Line bottom of pan with parchment paper. Butter parchment paper and sides of pan.

Step 3

Combine 1 tablespoon instant espresso powder and 1 tablespoon hot water in bowl; set aside.

Step 4

Place butter and chocolate in 2-quart nonstick saucepan. Cook over medium heat, stirring occasionally, until melted. Remove from heat; stir in espresso mixture. Add sugar; beat with whisk until combined. Add 1 egg at a time, whisking after each addition. Whisk in cocoa until well mixed.

Step 5

Pour cake into prepared pan. Place springform pan into center of large roasting pan. Place roasting pan in oven. Fill space around springform pan slowly with hot water, to about 1 inch up sides of pan. Bake 40-45 minutes or until center of cake is set.

Step 6

Remove springform pan from roasting pan. Place onto cooling rack; remove foil. Cool completely.

Step 7

Combine 1 teaspoon instant espresso powder and 1 teaspoon hot water in bowl; set aside.

Step 8

Beat chilled whipping cream and 1/4 cup sugar in chilled bowl at high speed, scraping bowl often, until stiff peaks form. Stir in espresso mixture.

Step 9

Combine powdered sugar and edible glitter in bowl.

Step 10

Remove sides from springform pan; place cake onto serving plate. Place snowflake stencil on top of cake (see Recipe Tips). Lightly dust top of cake with powdered sugar mixture. Carefully remove stencil.

Step 11

Serve with espresso whipped cream.

HAZELNUT AND CHIPPED CHOCOLATE CHEESECAKE

INGREDIENTS

- 2 cups semisweet chocolate chips
- 1 ½ cups vanilla wafer crumbs
- ¾ cup toasted, ground hazelnuts
- 2 tablespoons white sugar
- 3 tablespoons butter, melted
- 3 (8 ounce) packages cream cheese, softened
- 1 cup white sugar
- 3 large eggs eggs, beaten
- 3 tablespoons hazelnut liqueur
- 13 nuts skinned, toasted hazelnuts
- 4 tablespoons sour cream
- 1 tablespoon hazelnut liqueur

DIRECTIONS

Step 1

Using a blender or a food processor, finely chop 1/3 cup semisweet chocolate chips. Place in a small mixing bowl. Add vanilla wafer crumbs, ground hazelnuts, 2 tablespoons white sugar, and melted butter or margarine. Mix until well combined. Press onto the bottom and up the sides of a 9 inch springform pan. Bake in a preheated 300 degrees F (150 degrees C) oven for 15 minutes. Cool.

Step 2

In a large bowl, beat the cream cheese until fluffy. Gradually add 1 cup white sugar; mix well. Add the eggs and 3 tablespoons liqueur. Mix until well blended. Coarsely chop 1 cup of the semisweet chocolate chips, and add to the cream cheese mixture. Stir. Pour batter into the cooled crust.

Step 3

Bake in a preheated 350 degrees F (175 degrees C) oven for 1 hour. Let cake cool for 1 hour. Remove outer ring from pan. Then let cool completely.

Step 4

Melt 2/3 cup semisweet chocolate chips over hot (not boiling) water. Stir until smooth. Dip 13 hazelnuts into the chocolate, covering one-half of each nut. Shake off the excess chocolate. Place on a waxed-paper lined plate. Chill until set.

Step 5

To the remaining melted chocolate, add sour cream. Mix well. Stir in 1 tablespoon liqueur. Spread glaze on top of the cooled cheesecake. Garnish with chocolate dipped hazelnuts.

CHOCOLATE-STUFFED PANETTONE

INGREDIENTS

- 2 (1 pound) loaves panettone

Filling:

- 11 ounces 70% dark chocolate, chopped
- 1 cup heavy whipping cream
- 1 tablespoon brandy
- ¾ cup chopped walnuts

Glaze:

- 1 (5 ounce) milk chocolate, chopped
- 1 tablespoon chopped dried apricots, or more to taste
- 1 tablespoon chopped walnuts, or more to taste

DIRECTIONS

Step 1

Slice off the top parts of the panettone right under the dome with a serrated knife. Cut into the panettone, leaving a 1/2-inch border around the edges and bottom and scoop out the soft interior. Crumble up the interior into a bowl.

Step 2

Place dark chocolate and cream in top of a double boiler over simmering water. Stir frequently, scraping down the sides with a rubber spatula to avoid scorching, until chocolate is melted, about 5 minutes.

Remove from heat and stir in brandy. Fold in chopped walnuts and allow to cool for about 15 minutes. Combine chocolate mixture with panettone crumbs and mix well.

Step 3

Spoon chocolate-panettone mixture into the hollowed-out panettone. Hollow out and fill the lid if there's leftover filling. Cover stuffed panettone.

Step 4

Place milk chocolate in top of a double boiler over simmering water. Stir frequently, scraping down the sides with a rubber spatula to avoid scorching, until chocolate is melted, about 5 minutes. Drizzle melted chocolate over the top of the panettone and garnish with dried apricots and walnuts.

MINT DEVIL'S FOOD CUPCAKES

INGREDIENTS

Cupcakes:

- cooking spray
- ¼ cup unsalted butter
- 2 (1 ounce) squares semisweet chocolate
- 1 cup all-purpose flour
- 2 tablespoons all-purpose flour
- ¾ teaspoon baking soda
- ⅛ teaspoon salt
- 2 tablespoons milk
- ½ teaspoon distilled white vinegar
- ½ drop pure peppermint extract
- 1 cup white sugar
- 1 egg
- ½ cup boiling water

Whipped Cream Frosting:

- 2 tablespoons cold water, or more as needed
- 1 (.25 ounce) package unflavored gelatin
- 1 cup heavy whipping cream
- 3 tablespoons heavy whipping cream
- ¼ cup confectioners' sugar
- 2 teaspoons confectioners' sugar
- ½ teaspoon imitation vanilla extract
- 1 drop green food coloring
- 6 cookies chocolate sandwich cookies (such as Oreo)

DIRECTIONS

Step 1

Preheat oven to 350 degrees F (175 degrees C). Lightly spray 12 muffin cups.

Step 2

Heat butter and chocolate together in a small saucepan over low heat until melted, about 5 minutes. Remove from heat; set aside to cool slightly, about 5 minutes.

Step 3

Combine 1 cup plus 2 tablespoons flour, baking soda, and salt together in a small bowl.

Step 4

Mix milk, vinegar, and peppermint extract together in another small bowl.

Step 5

Beat sugar and eggs together in large bowl with an electric mixer on medium speed until pale, about 3 minutes. Add melted chocolate and beat well to combine. Pour in 1/2 cup boiling water and beat until batter is well-blended. Add flour mixture; beat on low speed until incorporated. Add milk mixture and blend well. Fill muffin cups 3/4-full with batter.

Step 6

Bake in the preheated oven until a toothpick inserted into a cupcake comes out clean, 25 to 30 minutes. Transfer cupcakes to wire rack and cool to room temperature, about 45 minutes.

Step 7

Combine 2 tablespoons cold water and gelatin in a small saucepan over low heat. Stir constantly until gelatin dissolves, about 5 minutes. Remove from heat and let cool slightly, but not until set, about 5 minutes.

Step 8

Combine 1 cup plus 3 tablespoons heavy cream, 1/4 cup plus 2 teaspoons confectioners' sugar, vanilla extract, and green food coloring in a large bowl. Whip with an electric mixer on low speed until slightly thickened, about 5 minutes. Beat in dissolved gelatin slowly. Increase speed to high and beat until frosting is stiff, about 3 minutes.

Step 9

Spread frosting over cooled cupcakes. Remove and discard cream filling from chocolate sandwich cookies; crush cookies. Scatter cookie crumbs over cupcakes.

SAUSAGE CHRISTMAS CAKE

INGREDIENTS

- 1 pound pork sausage
- 1 cup cold, brewed coffee
- 1 cup packed dark brown sugar
- 1 cup white sugar
- 2 large eggs eggs, beaten
- 1 teaspoon ground cinnamon
- 1 teaspoon ground nutmeg
- ½ teaspoon ground cloves
- 2 cups self-rising flour
- 1 cup chopped walnuts
- ½ cup golden raisins

- ½ cup raisins

DIRECTIONS

Step 1

Mix together cinnamon, nutmeg, cloves, and flour in a bowl.

Step 2

Add sausage, coffee, sugars, and eggs to the dry ingredients. Add raisins and nuts. Pour into an ungreased angel food cake pan.

Step 3

Bake in preheated oven at 350 degrees F (175 degrees C) for 1 hour or till a toothpick comes out clean.

Step 4

Garnishes may be added such as drizzled white frosting with whole cherries and mint leaves. This cake is so moist. If you like the flavor of rum you can wrap a rum-soaked damp cloth around it and refrigerate for several weeks. Best served with a spoonful of whipped cream.

EGGNOG-CHAI CUPCAKES

INGREDIENTS

Cupcakes:

- 1 (15.25 ounce) package spiced cake mix (such as Betty Crocker)
- 1 cup brewed chai tea
- ½ cup vegetable oil
- 3 large eggs eggs

Frosting:

- ½ cup butter, softened
- 1 (8 ounce) package cream cheese, softened
- 2 cups confectioners' sugar
- 1 teaspoon vanilla extract
- ½ teaspoon ground nutmeg
- 2 tablespoons eggnog
- 1 teaspoon rum extract

DIRECTIONS

Step 1

Preheat oven to 350 degrees F (175 degrees C). Line muffin cups with paper liners.

Step 2

Beat cake mix, chai tea, vegetable oil, and eggs together in a bowl using an electric mixer on low speed for 30 seconds. Increase speed to medium and beat until batter is smooth, about 2 minutes more. Spoon batter into the prepared muffin cups, filling 2/3-full.

Step 3

Bake in the preheated oven until a toothpick inserted in the center comes out clean, 22 to 24 minutes. Cool cupcakes in the tin for 5 minutes before transferring to a wire rack to cool completely.

Step 4

Beat butter and cream cheese together in a bowl using an electric mixer on medium speed until smooth, 20 to 30 seconds. Add confectioners' sugar, vanilla extract, and nutmeg and beat on medium-high speed until smooth, about 1 minute. Scrape sides of bowl as needed. Add eggnog and beat until fully incorporated into the frosting; beat in rum extract on medium-low speed.

Step 5

Transfer frosting to a pastry bag or plastic bag with a corner snipped and pipe frosting onto cooled cupcakes.

ELEGANT EASY TORTE

INGREDIENTS

- 1 (13 ounce) package frozen pound cake, thawed
- 1 (12.5 ounce) can cherry pie filling, or flavor of choice
- 8 ounces whipped topping
- ½ cup chopped nuts

DIRECTIONS

Step 1

Slice thawed pound cake horizontally into 3 layers. Spread bottom layer with pie filling, and top with center slice. Spread middle layer with whipped topping, and cover with last slice. Sprinkle with chopped nuts.

Step 2

Slice, and serve. Store in the refrigerator.

TRIPLE EGGNOG CAKE

INGREDIENTS

Cake:

- 1 (15.25 ounce) package yellow cake mix
- 1 ½ cups eggnog, or more to taste
- 2 large eggs eggs
- ¼ cup melted butter
- ½ teaspoon ground nutmeg
- ½ teaspoon rum-flavored extract

Filling:

- 2 cups eggnog
- 1 (3.5 ounce) package instant vanilla pudding mix
- ½ teaspoon rum-flavored extract

Topping:

- 2 tablespoons cold water
- 1 tablespoon unflavored gelatin
- 2 cups heavy whipping cream
- 1 ¼ cups white sugar
- ½ teaspoon rum-flavored extract
- 1 pinch salt

DIRECTIONS

Step 1

Preheat oven to 350 degrees F (175 degrees C). Grease 2 round cake pans.

Step 2

Mix cake mix, 1 1/2 cups eggnog, eggs, butter, nutmeg, and 1/2 teaspoon rum-flavored extract together in a bowl using an electric mixer until batter is smooth, about 4 minutes. Pour batter into the prepared pans.

Step 3

Bake in the preheated oven until a toothpick inserted in the center comes out clean, about 30 minutes. Remove cakes from pans and cool on a wire rack.

Step 4

Mix 2 cups eggnog, vanilla pudding mix, and 1/2 teaspoon rum-flavored extract together in a bowl until smooth; refrigerate until pudding thickens, at least 30 minutes.

Step 5

Mix cold water and gelatin together in a bowl until gelatin is dissolved. Beat cream in a separate bowl using an electric mixer until soft peaks form; add gelatin mixture, white sugar, 1/2 teaspoon rum-flavored extract, and salt and beat until stiff peaks form. Refrigerate topping until chilled, at least 30 minutes.

Step 6

Place 1 cake on a serving plate and spread 1/2 of the filling on top. Place the second cake over the filling and top with remaining filling. Cover entire cake with whipped cream topping. Store cake in refrigerator.

ORANGE CRUNCH BUNDT CAKE

INGREDIENTS

- 1 cup butter
- 1 cup white sugar
- 2 large eggs eggs
- 1 cup sour cream
- 2 cups all-purpose flour
- 1 teaspoon baking soda
- 1 cup raisins
- ½ cup walnuts
- 1 teaspoon vanilla extract

- 2 tablespoons orange zest
- ¼ cup orange juice
- ½ cup white sugar

DIRECTIONS

Step 1

Preheat oven to 350 degrees F (175 degrees C). Grease and flour a 10 inch bundt pan.

Step 2

Cream butter or margarine and 1 cup sugar. Add eggs, and beat well with an electric mixer at medium speed. Mix in sour cream and vanilla. Combine flour and baking soda: add to creamed mixture, blending just until moistened. Stir in raisins, walnuts, and orange rind. Mix well. Pour batter into prepared pan.

Step 3

Bake for 60 minutes, or until a wooden pick comes out clean. Cool cake in pan for 5 minutes.

Step 4

Dissolve 1/2 cup sugar in orange juice. Pour over hot cake. Cool completely in pan.

CHRISTMAS CHEESE CAKE

INGREDIENTS

- 1 (3 ounce) package ladyfinger cookies
- 3 (8 ounce) packages cream cheese
- 1 cup white sugar
- 4 large eggs eggs
- 1 ½ pints sour cream
- 1 tablespoon vanilla extract
- 1 tablespoon almond extract
- 1 (21 ounce) can cherry pie filling

DIRECTIONS

Step 1

Preheat oven to 375 degrees F (190 degrees C). Line the sides of one 10 inch springform pan with lady fingers then line the bottom with lady fingers (cutting lady fingers, if necessary).

Step 2

Cream the cream cheese and sugar together. Add the eggs, one at a time, beating after each addition. Stir in the extracts and fold in the sour cream. Pour batter into the prepared pan. Cover tops of lady fingers with foil.

Step 3

Bake at 375 degrees F (190 degrees C) for 50 to 60 minutes, until almost set in the middle. Remove cake from oven and let stand for 1/2 hour, then remove sides of pan. Place in the refrigerator for at least 24 hours. Before serving top with canned pie filling.

CARROT-OATMEAL SPICE CAKE

INGREDIENTS

- 1 cup raisins
- ⅓ cup shredded carrots
- 2 cups water
- 1 cup all-purpose flour
- 1 cup quick cooking oats
- 1 ½ teaspoons artificial sweetener
- ½ teaspoon salt
- 1 teaspoon baking soda
- 1 teaspoon ground cinnamon
- ½ cup margarine, softened
- ¼ cup egg substitute
- 1 teaspoon vanilla extract
- ⅓ cup pecans, coarsely chopped

DIRECTIONS

Step 1

Preheat oven to 350 degrees F (175 degrees C). Grease a 7x11 inch baking dish. Set aside.

Step 2

Combine raisins, carrots, and water in a medium saucepan. Bring to a boil, reduce heat and simmer for 10 minutes. Remove from heat and allow to cool.

Step 3

In a mixing bowl, combine flour, oatmeal, sugar substitute, salt, baking soda and cinnamon.

Step 4

In a separate bowl, mix together the margarine, egg substitute, and vanilla. Add to the flour mixture and mix well.

Step 5

Add the raisin mixture and nuts, mix well and pour into baking pan.

Step 6

Bake for 35 minutes or until toothpick inserted in middle comes out clean.

Santa Favorite Cake

INGREDIENTS

- 1 (18.25 ounce) package white cake mix
- 3 large egg whites egg whites
- 1 ⅓ cups buttermilk
- 2 tablespoons vegetable oil
- 1 (9 ounce) package yellow cake mix

- ½ cup buttermilk
- 1 egg
- 1 ½ tablespoons unsweetened cocoa powder
- 2 tablespoons red food coloring
- 1 teaspoon cider vinegar
- 1 (8 ounce) package cream cheese, softened
- 1 cup margarine, softened
- 2 (16 ounce) packages confectioners' sugar
- 2 teaspoons peppermint extra

DIRECTIONS

Step 1

Preheat oven to 350 degrees F (175 degrees C). Grease and flour three 9 inch round cake pans.

Step 2

In a large bowl, combine white cake mix, 3 egg whites, 1 1/3 cups buttermilk, and 2 tablespoons vegetable oil. Mix with an electric mixer for 2 minutes on high speed. In a separate bowl, combine yellow cake mix, 1/2 cup buttermilk, 1 egg, cocoa, red food coloring, and vinegar. Use an electric mixer to beat for 2 minutes on high speed.

Step 3

Spoon white batter alternately with red batter into the prepared cake pans. Swirl batter gently with a knife to create a marbled effect.

Step 4

Bake in preheated oven for 22 to 25 minutes, or until a wooden pick inserted into the centers comes out clean. Let cool in pans for at least 10 minutes before turning out onto a wire rack to cool completely.

Step 5

In a large bowl, beat cream cheese and margarine until smooth. Gradually blend in sugar until incorporated and smooth. Stir in peppermint extract. Spread peppermint cream cheese frosting between layers, and on top and sides of cake.

Cookie

PEPPERMINT MERINGUE COOKIES

INGREDIENTS

- 2 large egg whites egg whites
- ⅛ teaspoon cider vinegar
- ⅛ teaspoon salt
- ⅓ cup white sugar
- 3 eaches peppermint candy canes, crushed

DIRECTIONS

Step 1

Preheat the oven to 225 degrees F (110 degrees C). Line cookie sheets with aluminum foil or parchment paper.

Step 2

In a large glass or metal bowl, whip egg whites, vinegar and salt to soft peaks. Gradually add sugar while continuing to whip until stiff peaks form, about 5 minutes. Fold in 1/3 of the crushed candy canes, reserving the rest. Drop by heaping teaspoonfuls, one inch apart onto the prepared cookie sheets. Sprinkle remaining crushed candy canes over the top.

Step 3

Bake for 90 minutes in the preheated oven, or until dry. Cool on baking sheets.

PEBBER NODDER (DANISH CHRISTMAS COOKIES)

INGREDIENTS

- 1 cup butter
- 1 cup sugar
- 2 large eggs eggs
- 2 ½ cups all-purpose flour
- 1 teaspoon ground cardamom
- 1 teaspoon ground cinnamon, or to taste

DIRECTIONS

Step 1

Preheat the oven to 350 degrees F (175 degrees C).

Step 2

In a large bowl, mix together the butter and sugar until smooth. Beat in the eggs one at a time, stirring until light and fluffy. Combine the flour, cardamom and cinnamon; stir into the sugar mixture just until blended.

Step 3

Separate the dough into 6 balls, and roll each ball into a rope about as big around as your finger on a lightly floured surface. Cut into 1/2-inch pieces, and place them on an ungreased baking sheet.

Step 4

Bake for 10 minutes in the preheated oven, or until lightly browned. Cool on baking sheets for a few minutes, then transfer to wire racks to cool completely.

MANDELMAKRONEN (ALMOND MERINGUES)

INGREDIENTS

- 4 large egg whites egg whites
- 1 cup white sugar

- 1 ½ cups almond flour, or more as needed
- ¼ teaspoon ground cinnamon

DIRECTIONS

Step 1

Preheat oven to 300 degrees F (150 degrees C). Line 2 baking sheets with parchment paper.

Step 2

Beat egg whites in a glass, metal, or ceramic bowl until stiff peaks form. Gradually add sugar, 1 teaspoon at a time, while continuing to beat at high speed. Combine ground almonds and cinnamon in a bowl and fold into the egg white mixture with a spatula. Add more ground almonds if mixture is too runny.

Step 3

Use 2 teaspoons to place little mounds of almond mixture 2 inches apart onto the prepared baking sheets.

Step 4

Bake in the preheated oven until lightly browned and baked through, 15 to 20 minutes. Carefully remove from baking sheets and cool on wire racks.

GERMAN WALNUT SHORTBREAD COOKIES

INGREDIENTS

- ¾ cup unsalted butter, at room temperature
- 2 tablespoons unsalted butter, room temperature
- ¾ cup confectioners' sugar
- 4 teaspoons confectioners' sugar
- 1 egg yolk
- 1 pinch salt
- 2 ¼ cups all-purpose flour
- 2 tablespoons all-purpose flour
- ¾ cup chopped walnuts
- 2 tablespoons chopped walnuts

DIRECTIONS

Step 1

Beat 3/4 cup plus 2 tablespoons butter in a large bowl using an electric mixer until creamy. Add 3/4 cup plus 4 teaspoons confectioner's sugar, egg yolk, and salt; beat until smooth. Knead in 2 1/4 cups plus 2 tablespoons flour and 3/4 cup plus 2 tablespoons walnuts.

Step 2

Shape dough into 2-inch thick rolls and press them into rectangles using a flat item like a cutting board (they should look like oversized butter sticks). Wrap in plastic wrap and refrigerate until firm, about 1 hour.

Step 3

Preheat oven to 375 degrees F (190 degrees C).

Step 4

Cut dough into thin slices and lay them on an ungreased baking sheet.

Step 5

Bake in the preheated oven for 10 minutes. Reduce heat to 250 degrees F (120 degrees C) and bake until very lightly browned, about 5 more minutes.

Step 6

Remove from the baking sheet and cool on a wire rack, about 20 minutes.

LINZER TORTE COOKIES

INGREDIENTS

- ¾ cup butter, softened
- 1 cup white sugar
- 1 egg
- 1 teaspoon lemon zest
- 2 cups all-purpose flour
- ¾ cup blanched slivered almonds, ground
- 1 teaspoon ground cinnamon
- ⅛ teaspoon ground cloves
- 1 cup raspberry jam

DIRECTIONS

Step 1

Preheat oven to 350 degrees F (175 degrees C). Grease an 11x7 inch baking pan.

Step 2

In a medium bowl, cream together the butter and sugar. Beat in the egg and lemon peel. In another bowl, stir together the flour, almonds, cinnamon and cloves. Gradually stir the dry ingredients into the creamed mixture. The dough will be stiff, so you may need to knead it by hand to get it to come together. Press half of the dough into the bottom of the prepared pan.

Step 3

Press half of the dough into the bottom of the prepared pan. Spread the preserves over the crust. On a lightly floured surface, roll the remaining dough into long rope about 1/2 inch in diameter. Place lengths of the rope across the top of the jam in a lattice pattern over the preserves.

Step 4

Bake 40 minutes or until top is golden. Cool in pan on wire rack. Cut into 2 inch by 1inch bars.

EASY VEGAN GINGERBREAD COOKIES

INGREDIENTS

- 1 ½ cups all-purpose flour
- 1 teaspoon baking powder
- 1 teaspoon ground cinnamon
- ½ teaspoon baking soda
- ½ teaspoon ground ginger
- ½ teaspoon ground allspice
- ¼ teaspoon salt
- ½ cup coconut oil, at room temperature
- ⅓ cup molasses
- ¼ cup white sugar
- 1 teaspoon vanilla extract

DIRECTIONS

Step 1

Preheat oven to 350 degrees F (175 degrees C). Line 2 baking sheets with parchment paper.

Step 2

Sift flour, baking powder, cinnamon, baking soda, ginger, allspice, and salt into a bowl.

Step 3

Cream coconut oil, molasses, and sugar in a bowl with an electric mixer; add vanilla extract. Stir in flour mixture; mix until a sticky dough forms, about 2 minutes. Wrap dough in plastic wrap and chill for 2 hours.

Step 4

Roll out dough on a floured surface to 1/4 to 1/2-inch thickness. Dip cookie cutter in flour, cut out cookies, and place on the prepared baking sheets.

Step 5

Bake in the preheated oven until lightly golden, 8 to 10 minutes.

CLASSIC BUTTER COOKIES

INGREDIENTS

- 2 ½ cups all-purpose flour
- 1 cup butter
- ½ cup white sugar
- 1 egg
- ½ teaspoon almond extract

DIRECTIONS

Step 1

Cream the butter until light. Gradually add the sugar and beat until light and fluffy. Beat in the egg and almond extract.

Step 2

Gradually blend in the flour. Cover and chill dough for at least 1 hour.

Step 3

Preheat oven to 350 degrees F (175 degrees C).

Step 4

Roll dough out on a lightly floured surface to 1/8 inch thickness. Cut into desired shapes, using lightly floured cookie cutters. Place cookies on ungreased cookie sheets.

Step 5

Bake at 350 degrees F (175 degrees C) for 8 to 12 minutes or until golden. Remove to wire racks to cool completely. Decorate as desired.

CRAZY YUMMY CRANBERRY PECAN COOKIES WITH ORANGE GLAZE

INGREDIENTS

Cookie:

- 2 ¼ cups all-purpose flour
- 1 teaspoon baking soda
- 1 teaspoon salt
- 1 cup butter
- ¾ cup white sugar
- ¾ cup brown sugar, packed
- 1 teaspoon vanilla extract
- 2 large eggs eggs
- 1 cup chopped pecans
- 1 cup rolled oats
- 1 cup sweetened dried cranberries (such as Ocean Spray Craisins)

Glaze:

- 1 ½ cups confectioners' sugar
- ½ cup freshly squeezed orange juice
- 1 orange, zested
- 1 tablespoon butter

DIRECTIONS

Step 1

Preheat an oven to 375 degrees F (190 degrees C). Sift the flour, baking soda, and salt together in a bowl.

Step 2

In a large bowl, beat together the butter, white and brown sugars, and vanilla extract with an electric mixer until the mixture is creamy and well blended. Beat in eggs, one at a time, and then gradually beat in the flour just until the mixture makes a soft dough. Stir in the pecans, rolled oats, and cranberries, and drop by heaping spoonfuls onto ungreased baking sheets.

Step 3

Bake in the preheated oven until the cookies are set and the edges are slightly brown, 10 to 12 minutes. Let the cookies cool for 1 minute on baking sheets before removing to wire racks to finish cooling. Glaze cookies while still a little warm.

Step 4

Place the confectioners' sugar and orange juice in a microwave-safe bowl, and stir to dissolve the sugar. Stir in the orange zest and butter, and microwave on medium power until the butter melts and the mixture is warm, about 30 seconds. Stir the warm glaze until smooth, and drizzle over cookies.

CZECHOSLOVAKIAN COOKIES

Servings: 12 **Yield:** 2 dozen

INGREDIENTS

- 1 cup butter
- 1 cup white sugar
- 2 large egg yolks egg yolks
- 1 teaspoon vanilla extract
- ⅛ teaspoon ground cardamom
- ¼ teaspoon ground allspice
- 2 cups all-purpose flour
- 1 cup chopped pecans
- ½ cup strawberry jam

DIRECTIONS

Step 1

Preheat oven to 325 degrees F (165 degrees C). Grease one 8 inch square baking dish.

Step 2

Cream the butter until soft and fluffy. Add the white sugar gradually, until light and fluffy. Beat in the egg yolks.

Step 3

Sift the cardamom, allspice and flour together. Gradually add it to the butter mixture and stir to combine well. Stir in the chopped pecans.

Step 4

Spoon 1/2 of the dough into the prepared pan, spreading evenly. Top with strawberry jam and cover with the remaining dough.

Step 5

Bake at 325 degrees F (165 degrees C) for 1 hour or until lightly browned. Cool then cut into 1 1/2 inch sized squares.

CHINESE CHRISTMAS COOKIES

INGREDIENTS

- 1 cup semisweet chocolate chips
- 1 cup peanut butter chips
- 1 cup chow mein noodles
- 1 cup dry-roasted peanuts

DIRECTIONS

Step 1

Melt chocolate and peanut butter chips in the top of a double boiler over simmering water, stirring frequently, until smooth.

Step 2

Mix chow mein noodles and peanuts in a large mixing bowl. Pour chocolate mixture over noodles and peanuts and turn to coat.

Step 3

Line a baking sheet with waxed paper. Drop mixture by rounded tablespoonfuls onto prepared sheet. Refrigerate until set, about 2 hours.

CHEESECAKE TOPPED BROWNIES

INGREDIENTS

- 1 (21.5 ounce) package brownie mix
- 1 (8 ounce) package cream cheese, softened
- 2 tablespoons butter, softened
- 1 tablespoon cornstarch
- 1 (14 ounce) can sweetened condensed milk
- 1 egg
- 1 teaspoon vanilla extract
- 1 (16 ounce) container prepared chocolate frosting

DIRECTIONS

Step 1

Preheat oven 350 degrees F (175 degrees C). Grease a 9x13 inch baking pan.

Step 2

Prepare brownie mix according to the directions on the package. Spread into prepared baking pan.

Step 3

In a medium bowl, beat cream cheese, butter and cornstarch until fluffy. Gradually beat in sweetened condensed milk, egg and vanilla until smooth. Pour cream cheese mixture evenly over brownie batter.

Step 4

Bake in preheated oven for 45 minutes, or until top is lightly browned. Allow to cool, spread with frosting, and cut into bars. Store covered in refrigerator, or freeze in a single layer for up to 2 weeks.

CHOCOLATE CANTUCCI

INGREDIENTS

- 1 ¼ cups white sugar
- 3 eaches eggs
- 1 teaspoon vanilla extract
- 2 ½ cups all-purpose flour
- 2 teaspoons baking powder
- ¾ cup chopped dark chocolate

DIRECTIONS

Step 1

Preheat oven to 350 degrees F (175 degrees C). Line a baking sheet with parchment paper.

Step 2

Combine sugar, eggs, and vanilla extract in a large bowl; beat with an electric mixer until frothy. Add flour and baking powder and mix well. Fold in chocolate pieces until a sticky dough forms. Separate dough into 2 portions and shape each portion into a long, thick log. Place logs 2 inches apart on the prepared baking sheet.

Step 3

Bake logs in the preheated oven until golden brown, 15 to 20 minutes.

Step 4

Remove logs from the oven and cool until easily handled, about 5 minutes. Transfer to a cutting board; slice logs diagonally into 3/4-inch slices using a serrated knife.

Step 5

Return cantucci slices to the baking sheet and return to the oven. Turn off oven and allow cantucci to dry in the warm oven for 30 minutes. Cool to room temperature, about 10 minutes, before serving.

CINNAMON STARS

Servings: 18 **Yield:** 3 dozen

INGREDIENTS

- 2 ⅔ cups finely ground almonds
- 1 tablespoon ground cinnamon
- 1 teaspoon lemon zest
- ⅓ cup egg whites
- ⅛ teaspoon salt
- 2 ½ cups confectioners' sugar
- 1 ¾ teaspoons lemon juice

DIRECTIONS

Step 1

Stir together the almonds, cinnamon, and lemon zest until combined.

Step 2

Beat the egg whites and salt until soft peaks form. Slowly sift in the confectioner's sugar, continuing to beat until the mixture is stiff. Set aside 1/3 cup of the egg white mixture for the glaze. Fold in the almond mixture.

Step 3

Preheat oven to 325 degrees F (170 degrees C). Line the cookie sheets with parchment paper.

Step 4

Roll the dough to 1/4 inch thickness on a surface that has been sprinkled with confectioners' sugar. Using a 2 1/2-inch star cookie cutter, cut out the cookies and place them on the cookie sheets.

Step 5

To make the glaze, add the lemon juice to the reserved egg white mixture, stirring until smooth. Brush the tops of the cookies lightly with the glaze. (If the glaze starts to thicken, add a few more drops of lemon juice.)

Step 6

Bake for 20 to 25 minutes. When done, they will be light brown and soft in the center. Remove and cool on wire racks.

CHOCOLATE PECAN PIE BARS

INGREDIENTS

Crust:

- 2 cups all-purpose flour
- ⅓ cup white sugar
- ⅓ teaspoon salt
- ⅔ cup margarine

Filling:

- 1 ½ cups light corn syrup (such as Karo)
- 1 cup brown sugar
- 4 large eggs eggs
- 3 tablespoons margarine
- 1 ½ teaspoons vanilla extract
- ⅛ teaspoon salt
- 1 ½ cups chopped pecans
- 1 (11 ounce) package chocolate chips

DIRECTIONS

Step 1

Preheat the oven to 350 degrees F (175 degrees C). Lightly grease a 10x15-inch jelly roll pan.

Step 2

Stir flour, white sugar, and salt together in a large bowl. Cut in 2/3 cup margarine until mixture resembles coarse crumbs. Press mixture into the bottom of the prepared pan.

Step 3

Bake in the preheated oven for 20 minutes.

Step 4

While the crust is baking, prepare the filling by mixing corn syrup, brown sugar, eggs, margarine, vanilla extract, and salt together in a large bowl until smooth. Stir in pecans.

Step 5

Remove the crust from the oven and sprinkle with chocolate chips. Spread filling evenly over the chocolate chip covered crust.

Step 6

Bake in the preheated oven until set, 20 to 25 minutes. Cool completely before cutting into squares.

RED VELVET CHOCOLATE CHIP COOKIES

INGREDIENTS

- 1 ½ cups all-purpose flour
- ⅓ cup unsweetened cocoa powder
- 1 teaspoon baking soda
- ½ teaspoon baking powder
- ½ teaspoon salt
- ½ cup butter, softened
- ¾ cup brown sugar
- ¼ cup white sugar
- 1 egg
- 1 ½ tablespoons milk
- 1 ½ teaspoons vanilla extract
- 2 tablespoons red food coloring
- 1 cup dark chocolate chips, or as needed

DIRECTIONS

Step 1

Whisk flour, cocoa powder, baking soda, baking powder, and salt together in a bowl.

Step 2

Beat butter with an electric mixer until fluffy, about 2 minutes; beat in brown sugar and white sugar until smooth, about 1 minute. Beat egg, milk, and vanilla extract into butter mixture; beat in food coloring until uniformly colored.

Step 3

Stir flour mixture into butter mixture gradually with electric mixer on low speed until combined; stir in 1 cup chocolate chips. Cover bowl with plastic wrap; place in the refrigerator for 1 hour or up to overnight.

Step 4

Preheat oven to 350 degrees F (175 degrees C). Line baking sheets with parchment paper.

Step 5

Roll dough into 2-inch balls; place on prepared baking sheets and flatten slightly.

Step 6

Bake in the preheated oven until edges are lightly browned, about 10 minutes. Sprinkle cookies with a few additional chocolate chips; allow to cool completely.

GLUTEN-FREE GINGERSNAP COOKIES

INGREDIENTS

- ¾ cup unsalted butter, softened
- ½ cup brown sugar
- ½ cup unbleached cane sugar
- 1 egg
- ¼ cup blackstrap molasses
- 1 teaspoon vanilla extract
- 1 cup oat flour
- ½ cup almond flour
- ⅓ cup coconut flour
- 1 (1/4 inch thick) slice fresh ginger, grated
- 1 tablespoon ground ginger
- 1 teaspoon baking soda
- 1 teaspoon ground cinnamon
- 1 teaspoon ground nutmeg
- ½ teaspoon ground cloves
- ¼ cup unbleached cane sugar, or as needed
- ½ teaspoon ground cinnamon, or as needed
- ¼ teaspoon ground nutmeg, or as needed

DIRECTIONS

Step 1

Beat butter, brown sugar, and 1/2 cup cane sugar together in a bowl using an electric mixer until creamy. Add egg and mix to combine. Mix in molasses and vanilla extract.

Step 2

Mix oat flour, almond flour, coconut flour, fresh ginger, ground ginger, baking soda, 1 teaspoon cinnamon, 1 teaspoon nutmeg, and cloves together in a separate bowl. Add to butter mixture slowly and combine. Refrigerate dough for at least 1 hour, to overnight; dough will be very wet before it's chilled.

Step 3

Preheat the oven to 350 degrees F (175 degrees C). Line 2 large baking sheets with parchment paper.

Step 4

Combine 1/4 cup cane sugar, 1/2 teaspoon cinnamon, and 1/4 teaspoon nutmeg in a shallow dish.

Step 5

Scoop dough by tablespoonfuls and roll into balls. Roll balls in cinnamon-sugar mixture to coat and place onto the prepared baking sheets, making sure not to overcrowd as they will flatten and spread.

Step 6

Bake in the preheated oven until set and golden, 10 to 12 minutes. Let cookies sit for 5 minutes before transferring to a wire rack to cool. Serve warm or let cool completely before storing in an airtight container.

CHILDREN'S GINGERBREAD HOUSE

INGREDIENTS

- ¾ cup butter
- ⅞ cup packed light brown sugar
- 1 teaspoon lemon zest
- 1 ½ tablespoons lemon juice
- ½ cup molasses
- 2 large eggs eggs
- 3 cups all-purpose flour
- 2 teaspoons baking powder
- 1 tablespoon ground ginger
- 2 teaspoons ground allspice
- 6 large egg whites egg whites
- 4 (16 ounce) packages confectioners' sugar, sifted

DIRECTIONS

Step 1

First cut out in thin cardboard: a side wall, 4 1/2 x 8 inches; an end wall, 4 1/2x5 inches; a triangular gable, 4 1/2x3x3 inches; and a roof rectangle, 4 1/2x9 inches. Tape the rectangular end wall piece to the triangular gable piece: match the long side of the triangle, 4 1/2 inches, to one of the 4 1/2 inch sides of the end wall.

Step 2

In a large bowl, cream butter and sugar until light and fluffy. Stir in lemon zest, lemon juice, and molasses. Gradually beat in 2 eggs. Sift the flour, baking powder, and spices together; stir into creamed mixture. Wrap dough in parchment paper, and refrigerate for 1 hour.

Step 3

Turn out dough onto a lightly floured surface. Divide into 6 portions, 2 slightly larger than the others. On a lightly floured surface, roll out the 4 smaller pieces to approximately the size of the side wall and the end wall with gable templates; cut out two of each. Roll out remaining dough, and cut into two rectangular roof pieces. Transfer gingerbread onto greased baking trays.

Step 4

In a preheated 375 degree F (190 degrees C) oven, bake gingerbread for 10 minutes, or until crisp. When removing from the oven, leave the gingerbread on the baking trays for a few minutes to set, then transfer to wire racks. Leave out overnight to harden.

Step 5

In a large bowl, lightly whisk 2 egg whites. Gradually beat in approximately 5 cups confectioners' sugar. The icing should be smooth and stand in firm peaks. Spread or pipe a 9 inch line of icing onto a cake board, and press in one of the side walls so that it sticks firmly and stands upright. If necessary, spread or pipe a little extra icing along either side to help support it. Take an end wall and ice both the side edges. Spread or pipe a line of icing on the board at a right angle to the first wall, and press the end wall into position. Repeat this process with the other two walls until they are all in position. Leave the walls to harden together for at least two hours before putting on the roof. Spread or pipe a thick layer of icing on top of all the walls, and fix the roof pieces in position; the roof should overlap the walls to make the eaves. Pipe or spread a little icing along the crest of the roof to hold the two pieces firmly together. Leave overnight to set firmly.

Step 6

When ready to decorate, make the remaining icing. In a large bowl, lightly whisk 4 egg whites, and mix in remaining confectioners' sugar as before. Use this to make snow on the roof, and to stick various candies for decoration. Finish with a fine dusting of sifted confectioners' sugar.

ICELANDIC PEPPER COOKIES

Servings: 18 **Yield:** 3 dozen

INGREDIENTS

- 1 ¼ cups butter, softened
- 1 ¼ cups white sugar
- ¾ cup light corn syrup
- 2 small eggs
- 3 cups all-purpose flour
- 1 ½ teaspoons baking powder
- 1 teaspoon baking soda
- ½ teaspoon salt
- 2 teaspoons ground cinnamon
- 2 teaspoons ground cloves
- 1 teaspoon ground ginger
- ¼ teaspoon ground black pepper

DIRECTIONS

Step 1

In a large bowl, cream butter and sugar. Stir in corn syrup and eggs; cream well. Sift together flour, baking powder, baking soda, salt, cinnamon, cloves, ginger, and pepper. Add dry ingredients to the butter mixture, and mix until smooth. Refrigerate dough over night.

Step 2

Preheat oven to 350 degrees F (175 degrees C).

Step 3

Roll out dough to 1/4 inch thickness. Cut out cookies with a 2 inch round cookie cutter. Place at least 1 inch apart on cookie sheet and bake for 8 to 10 minutes in preheated oven.

RAISIN BUTTER TART SQUARES

INGREDIENTS

- 1 cup raisins
- 1 cup hot water, or as needed

Crust:

- 1 ½ cups all-purpose flour
- ½ cup butter, softened
- ¼ cup packed brown sugar

Filling:

- 1 cup brown sugar
- ⅓ cup butter, softened
- 1 egg
- 1 teaspoon vanilla extract
- 1 teaspoon heavy whipping cream
- 1 tablespoon all-purpose flour

DIRECTIONS

Step 1

Preheat oven to 325 degrees F (165 degrees C).

Step 2

Place raisins in a cup; pour in hot water to cover, and set aside to soak, about 5 minutes.

Step 3

Place 1 1/2 cups flour in a large bowl; cut in 1/2 cup butter until crumbly. Stir 1/4 cup brown sugar into flour mixture; press mixture evenly into the bottom of a 9x9-inch pan.

Step 4

Bake in the preheated oven until lightly browned, about 15 minutes. Remove from oven, leaving oven on.

Step 5

Beat 1 cup brown sugar and 1/3 cup butter together until smooth; stir in egg, vanilla extract, and cream. Strain raisins; stir raisins and 1 tablespoon flour into butter mixture. Pour raisin mixture over crust.

Step 6

Bake in the preheated oven until filling is bubbly, about 20 minutes. Allow to cool before cutting into squares, about 30 minutes.

NORWEGIAN BUTTER COOKIES

Servings: 12 **Yield:** 1 dozen

INGREDIENTS

- ½ cup butter
- 2 large eggs eggs
- ¼ cup white sugar
- 1 cup all-purpose flour
- ½ teaspoon vanilla extract

DIRECTIONS

Step 1

Preheat oven to 375 degrees F (190 degrees C).

Step 2

Hard boil the eggs and separate the yolks. Cream the butter and hard boiled egg yolks. Beat in the sugar and add the flour vanilla extract. Mix thoroughly. Put through a cookie press or arrange by teaspoonfuls on ungreased cookie sheets.

Step 3

Bake 10 to 12 minutes, or until lightly browned.

EGGNOG THUMBPRINTS

INGREDIENTS

- ¾ cup butter, softened
- ½ cup white sugar
- ¼ cup packed brown sugar
- 1 egg
- ½ teaspoon vanilla extract
- 2 cups all-purpose flour
- ¼ teaspoon salt
- ¼ cup butter
- 1 cup confectioners' sugar
- 1 tablespoon rum
- 1 pinch ground nutmeg

DIRECTIONS

Step 1

Preheat the oven to 350 degrees F (175 degrees C).

Step 2

In a medium bowl, cream together 3/4 cup butter, white sugar, and brown sugar until smooth. Beat in egg and vanilla. Combine flour and salt; stir into the creamed mixture by hand to form a soft dough. Roll dough into 1 inch balls, and place balls 2 inches apart on ungreased cookie sheets. Make an indention in the center of each cookie using your finger or thumb.

Step 3

Bake for 12 minutes in preheated oven. Cool completely.

Step 4

In a small bowl, mix together 1/4 cup butter, confectioners' sugar, and rum. Spoon rounded teaspoonfuls of filling onto cookies. Sprinkle with nutmeg. Let stand until set before storing in an airtight container.

STORYBOOK GINGERBREAD MEN

INGREDIENTS

- ½ cup shortening
- ½ cup packed brown sugar
- 3 ¼ cups sifted all-purpose flour
- 1 teaspoon salt
- 1 teaspoon baking soda
- ½ teaspoon ground cinnamon
- ½ teaspoon ground ginger
- ¾ cup molasses
- ¼ cup water

DIRECTIONS

Step 1

Cream shortening and sugar. Sift flour with salt, soda and spices. Blend flour mixture into creamed mixture alternately with molasses and water. Chill at least 1 hour.

Step 2

Preheat oven to 350 degrees F (180 degrees C).

Step 3

Roll dough to 1/4 inch thick. Cut with large 6-8 inch gingerbread men cookie cutters. Lift onto lightly greased cookie sheet with broad spatula.

Step 4

Bake above oven center for about 12 minutes or until cookies spring back lightly in center. Do not overcook, they won't stay soft. Remove from sheets. Cool on wire racks. Makes 10 men 6-8 inches tall.

NO-BAKE CHOCOLATE PEANUT BUTTER BARS

INGREDIENTS

- 2 cups peanut butter, divided
- ¾ cup butter, softened
- 2 cups powdered sugar
- 3 cups graham cracker crumbs
- 1 (12 ounce) package NESTLE TOLL HOUSE Semi-Sweet Chocolate Mini Morsels, divided

DIRECTIONS

Step 1

Grease 13 x 9-inch baking pan.

Step 2

Beat 1 1/4 cups peanut butter and butter in large mixer bowl until creamy. Gradually beat in 1 cup powdered sugar. With hands or wooden spoon, work in remaining powdered sugar, graham cracker crumbs and 1/2 cup morsels. Press evenly into prepared baking pan. Smooth top with spatula.

Step 3

Melt remaining peanut butter and remaining morsels in medium, heavy-duty saucepan over lowest possible heat, stirring constantly, until smooth. Spread over graham cracker crust in pan. Refrigerate for at least 1 hour or until chocolate is firm; cut into bars. Store in refrigerator.

MOM'S NUT HORNS

INGREDIENTS

Dough:

- ½ pound butter
- 2 cups all-purpose flour
- ¾ cup sour cream
- 1 egg yolk

Filling:

- ¾ cup finely ground walnuts
- ¾ cup white sugar
- 1 teaspoon ground cinnamon

DIRECTIONS

Step 1

Cut butter into flour in a bowl using 2 knives or a pastry blender until the mixture resembles coarse crumbs. Add sour cream and egg yolk; mix well. Shape the dough into a ball. Wrap in plastic wrap and refrigerate, 8 hours to overnight.

Step 2

Combine walnuts, sugar, and cinnamon in a small bowl.

Step 3

Preheat oven to 350 degrees F (175 degrees C). Lightly grease 2 baking sheets.

Step 4

Cut dough into 4 equal pieces. Roll each piece into a 1/8-inch thick circle on a lightly floured surface. Spread 1/4 of the walnut mixture on each circle; cut each circle into 12 wedge-shaped pieces with a pizza wheel.

Step 5

Shape each piece of dough into a crescent by rolling dough from the wide end of the wedge into the center. Transfer cookies carefully to the baking sheets.

Step 6

Bake in the preheated oven until golden, 20 to 25 minutes. Watch cookies carefully as they bake; their bottoms tend to brown faster than their tops.

SPRITZ COOKIES

Servings: 24 **Yield:** 4 dozen

INGREDIENTS

- 1 cup butter, softened
- 3 large egg yolks egg yolks
- 2 ½ cups all-purpose flour
- ⅔ cup white sugar
- 1 teaspoon vanilla extract

DIRECTIONS

Step 1

Mix the butter or margarine, sugar, egg yolks and vanilla. Add the flour and mix by hand.

Step 2

Spoon into cookie press and press onto ungreased cookie sheets. Sprinkle with colored sugars.

Step 3

Bake in preheated 400 degrees F (200 degrees C) oven for 7-10 minutes.

GINGERBREAD COOKIES

INGREDIENTS

- 1 ½ cups dark molasses
- 1 cup packed brown sugar
- ⅔ cup cold water
- ⅓ cup shortening
- 7 cups all-purpose flour
- 2 teaspoons baking soda
- 1 teaspoon salt
- 1 teaspoon ground allspice
- 2 teaspoons ground ginger
- 1 teaspoon ground cloves
- 1 teaspoon ground cinnamon
- 1 (16 ounce) package chocolate frosting

DIRECTIONS

Step 1

Preheat the oven to 350 degrees F (175 degrees C). Lightly grease one cookie sheet.

Step 2

Mix together the molasses, brown sugar, water and shortening.

Step 3

Sift together the flour, baking soda, salt, allspice, ginger, cloves and cinnamon. Add to sugar mixture and mix well. Cover and refrigerate for 2 hours.

Step 4

Roll dough 1/4 inch thick on floured board. Cut with floured gingerbread cutter. Place about 2 inches apart on cookie sheet. Bake for 10-12 minutes. Cool and decorate with frosting.

SHORTBREAD COOKIES

Servings: 12 **Yield:** 2 dozen

INGREDIENTS

- 1 cup butter, softened
- ½ cup confectioners' sugar
- ½ teaspoon salt
- ⅛ teaspoon ground nutmeg
- 1 egg yolk
- 2 cups all-purpose flour
- 1 (2.25 ounce) jar red decorator sugar
- 1 (10 ounce) jar maraschino cherries, drained

DIRECTIONS

Step 1

Preheat oven to 350 degrees F (175 degrees C).

Step 2

Cream together the butter, sugar, salt, nutmeg and egg yolk. Add the flour a little at a time until mixture is stiff.

Step 3

Place onto floured board and knead lightly until the dough begins to crack. Roll out 1/4 inch thickness and cut into desired shapes.

Step 4

Place on un-greased cookie sheet, decorate with colored sugar crystals and maraschino cherries.

Step 5

Bake for 10 minutes or until golden brown.

CHRISTMAS TREE MINI CUPCAKES

INGREDIENTS

Cupcakes:

- 1 ½ cups pastry flour
- 1 cup white sugar
- ⅓ cup cocoa powder
- 1 cup water

- ½ cup vegetable oil
- 1 teaspoon vanilla extract

Toppings:

- 1 cup vanilla frosting, or as desired
- 1 drop green food coloring, or as desired
- 48 small strawberries, hulled
- ¼ cup round red candies, or as desired
- star-shaped candies

DIRECTIONS

Step 1

Preheat oven to 350 degrees F (175 degrees C). Grease mini muffin cups or line with paper liners.

Step 2

Mix pastry flour, white sugar, and cocoa powder together in a bowl; add water, oil, and vanilla extract and blend until batter is smooth. Spoon batter into the prepared muffin cups.

Step 3

Bake in the preheated oven until a toothpick inserted in the center comes out clean, 8 to 12 minutes. Cool in the tin for 5 minutes.

Step 4

Mix frosting and green food coloring together in a bowl until evenly combined. Transfer frosting to a pipe bag or plastic bag with a snipped corner; refrigerate for 5 minutes.

Step 5

Squeeze a small amount of frosting onto the hulled side of each strawberry and place each onto a cupcake so the strawberry is in the shape of a tree. Pipe frosting onto each strawberry to look like leaves. Add candies to the "tree" to look like ornaments and place a star-shaped candy on top of each "tree".

NO-BAKE RAISIN CHEESECAKE

INGREDIENTS

- ¼ cup golden raisins
- ¼ cup raisins
- 1 cup plain low-fat yogurt
- 1 (3 ounce) package cream cheese
- 1 ¼ cups low-fat cottage cheese
- 1 teaspoon vanilla extract
- ½ cup white sugar
- ½ cup low-fat milk
- 1 (.25 ounce) package unflavored gelatin
- 3 large egg whites egg whites
- 1 cup boiling water
- 2 tablespoons water

DIRECTIONS

Step 1

Put all the raisins in a small bowl, and pour hot water over them. Set the bowl aside.

Step 2

Heat 1/4 cup white sugar with 2 tablespoons water in a small saucepan over medium-high heat. Boil the mixture until the bubbles rise to the surface in a random pattern. This indicates that the water has nearly evaporated, and that the sugar is beginning to cook. With a small spoon, drop a bit of the sugar into a bowl filled with ice water. If the sugar dissolves immediately, continue cooking the sugar mixture. Remove from heat when the sugar dropped into the water can be rolled between your fingers into a ball.

Step 3

Begin beating the egg whites with an electric mixer on high speed. Pour the sugar syrup down the side of the bowl in a thin, steady stream. When all the sugar has been incorporated, decrease mixer speed to medium. Continue beating until the egg whites are glossy, have formed stiff peaks, and have cooled to room temperature--about 10 minutes. Increase the speed to high, and beat the meringue for 1 minute more.

Step 4

Puree the yogurt, cream cheese, cottage cheese, vanilla extract, and 1/4 cup white sugar in a food processor or blender. Scrape the cheese mixture into a large bowl.

Step 5

Pour the milk into a small saucepan. Sprinkle the gelatin over the milk. Let it stand until the gelatin softens, about 5 minutes. Heat the milk over a medium heat, stirring until the gelatin is dissolved. Stir the milk into the cheese mixture. Mix about 1/3 of the meringue into the cheese mixture to lighten it. Gently fold in the rest of the meringue.

Step 6

Line an 8 inch cake pan with plastic wrap. Drain the raisins, and scatter them in the bottom of the pan. Then pour the cheesecake batter into the lined pan. Chill for 4 hours. To turn out the cheesecake, invert a serving plate on top of the pan. Turn both over together. Lift away the pan, peel off the plastic wrap, and slice for serving.

CARROT PUDDING

Servings: 8 **Yield:** 8 servings

INGREDIENTS

- ½ cup butter
- 1 cup white sugar
- 1 tablespoon minced carrot
- 1 cup peeled and shredded potatoes
- 1 cup all-purpose flour
- 2 cups raisins
- salt to taste
- 1 teaspoon ground cinnamon

- ¼ teaspoon ground nutmeg
- 1 teaspoon baking soda
- ½ cup green apples
- ½ cup white sugar
- 1 ½ tablespoons cornstarch
- 1 cup water
- 2 tablespoons butter
- 1 ½ tablespoons lemon juice

DIRECTIONS

Step 1

Cream 1/2 cup butter or margarine and 1 cup sugar. Mix in carrots, potatoes, and raisins. Sift flour, baking soda, salt, and spices together; mix into the creamed mixture. Stir in apples.

Step 2

Fill cans 2/3 full with pudding mixture. Cover with foil.

Step 3

Place cans in a roasting pan with 2 to 3 inches of water. Steam at 300 degrees F (150 degrees C) for 2 1/2 to 3 hours.

Step 4

Stir together 1/2 cup sugar and cornstarch. Combine mixture with water in a saucepan. Cook and stir over low heat until thick. Stir in 2 tablespoons butter or margarine and lemon juice. Serve warm over pudding.

STEAMED CURRANT CAKE

INGREDIENTS

- ¾ cup all-purpose flour
- ½ teaspoon ground cinnamon
- ½ teaspoon ground nutmeg
- 1 teaspoon baking soda
- ½ teaspoon salt
- 1 cup lard
- ¾ cup white sugar
- 2 large eggs eggs, beaten
- 1 cup chopped walnuts
- ⅔ cup chopped raisins
- ⅔ cup dried currants
- ⅔ cup chopped dates
- 1 cup fresh bread crumbs
- ½ cup orange juice
- 2 tablespoons butter
- ¾ cup confectioners' sugar
- ⅛ cup boiling water

- ⅛ cup brandy

DIRECTIONS

Step 1

Grease and flour a 9x5 inch loaf pan and line bottom with parchment paper. Sift together the flour, cinnamon, nutmeg, baking soda and salt. Set aside. Place a rack in the bottom of a large pot, over medium heat, and fill to the top of the rack with boiling water.

Step 2

In a large bowl cream the lard and sugar until fluffy. Beat in the eggs. Mix in the walnuts, chopped raisins, currants, dates, bread crumbs, and orange juice. Stir in the flour mixture until smooth. Pour into prepared pan.

Step 3

Cover the top with 2 layers of parchment paper and tie down with string. Place the pan on the rack. Cover pot and steam cake for 3 hours. Make sure to add water as it evaporates. Serve warm with Hard Sauce.

Step 4

To make the Hard Sauce: In a saucepan cream 2 tablespoons butter and 3/4 cup confectioners' sugar. Add 1/8 cup boiling water and 1/8 cup brandy. Cook, stirring, until clear and pour over individual servings.

CHOCOLATE-PEPPERMINT ROLL

INGREDIENTS

- 5 large egg whites egg whites
- 1 cup white sugar, divided
- 5 large egg yolks egg yolks
- ¼ teaspoon salt
- ¾ cup all-purpose flour
- ¼ cup cocoa powder
- ⅛ cup powdered sugar, or as needed
- 1 ½ pints peppermint ice cream

DIRECTIONS

Step 1

Preheat the oven to 350 degrees F (175 degrees C). Line a shallow 11x5-inch baking pan with greased waxed paper.

Step 2

Beat egg whites using an electric mixer in a mixing bowl until light and fluffy. Gradually add 1/2 cup white sugar and beat until combined.

Step 3

Beat egg yolks and salt together using an electric mixer in a separate bowl until light and fluffy. Gradually add remaining 1/2 cup sugar and beat until combined. Fold in egg white mixture. Fold in flour and cocoa powder. Pour batter into the prepared pan.

Step 4

Bake in the preheated oven until a toothpick inserted into the center comes out clean, about 25 minutes.

Step 5

Remove from the oven and turn cake onto a towel sprinkled heavily with powdered sugar. Remove waxed paper from cake and form into a roll. Let stand for about 4 minutes.

Step 6

Unroll cake and spread evenly with peppermint ice cream. Re-roll and freeze until ready to serve.

BEST CHRISTMAS CRANBERRY TORTE

INGREDIENTS

Graham Cracker Crust:

- 1 ½ cups graham cracker crumbs
- ½ cup chopped pecans
- ¼ cup white sugar
- 6 tablespoons butter, melted

Filling:

- 2 cups fresh cranberries, ground
- 1 cup white sugar
- 2 large egg whites pasteurized egg whites
- 1 tablespoon frozen orange juice concentrate, thawed
- 1 teaspoon vanilla extract
- ⅛ teaspoon salt
- 1 cup whipping cream

Cranberry Glaze:

- ½ cup white sugar
- 1 tablespoon cornstarch
- ¾ cup fresh cranberries
- ⅔ cup water
- 1 orange, sliced, or as needed

DIRECTIONS

Step 1

Combine graham cracker crumbs, pecans, sugar, and butter in a mixing bowl for crust. Press into the bottom and up the sides of an 8-inch springform pan. Chill.

Step 2

Meanwhile, combine cranberries and sugar for filling in a large mixing bowl. Let stand for 5 minutes. Add egg whites, orange juice, vanilla extract, and salt. Beat using an electric mixer on low speed until frothy. Beat on high until stiff peaks form (when the tips stand straight), 6 to 8 minutes.

Step 3

Whip cream in a small mixing bowl until soft peaks (or until the tips curl over); fold into cranberry mixture. Turn into crust and freeze until firm, 8 hours to overnight.

Step 4

Stir sugar and cornstarch for glaze together in a saucepan. Stir in cranberries and water. Cook and stir over medium-low heat until bubbly, about 5 minutes. Continue to cook, stirring occasionally, just until cranberry skins pop, about 5 minutes. Let cool to room temperature, about 30 minutes; do not chill.

Step 5

Remove torte from the pan. Place on a serving plate. Spoon cranberry glaze in the center; place orange slices around the outside.

POUSSE CAFÉ

Servings: 12 **Yield:** 1 fluted 2 quart ring mold

INGREDIENTS

- 2 ¼ cups pastry flour
- ½ teaspoon salt
- 2 ½ teaspoons baking powder
- ¾ cup shortening
- 1 ½ cups white sugar
- 3 large eggs eggs
- 1 teaspoon vanilla extract
- 3 tablespoons cognac
- ½ cup milk
- ½ cup light cream
- 2 cups heavy whipping cream
- ¼ cup white sugar
- 1 teaspoon instant coffee granules
- 1 tablespoon cognac

DIRECTIONS

Step 1

Preheat oven to 350 degrees F (175 degrees C). Grease thoroughly a fluted 2 quart ring mold, and dust lightly with flour.

Step 2

Sift pastry flour, salt, and baking powder together.

Step 3

In a large bowl, cream shortening well. Gradually blend in 1 1/2 cups sugar, eggs, vanilla, and 3 tablespoons cognac; beat until light and fluffy. Gently blend sifted ingredients alternately with the milk and cream into the creamed mixture. Pour batter into ring mold.

Step 4

Bake for 45 to 50 minutes, or until cake springs back when lightly touched. Remove from pan, and allow to cool.

Step 5

In a clean, cold bowl, beat the 2 cups whipping cream until peaks form. Stir in 1/4 cup sugar and coffee powder. Frost the cake with whipped cream. When serving, drizzle cake with a few drops of cognac.

PUMPKIN SPICE RING

INGREDIENTS

- 1 (18.25 ounce) package angel food cake mix
- 1 cup pumpkin puree
- ½ teaspoon pumpkin pie spice

DIRECTIONS

Step 1

Combine pumpkin and pumpkin pie spice, and mix well. Set aside.

Step 2

Mix cake as directed on package. Fold in pumpkin mixture. Pour into an ungreased tube pan.

Step 3

Bake at 350 degrees F (175 degrees C) until lightly browned, using the box directions as a guide to cooking time.

HOT MILK SPONGE CAKE

INGREDIENTS

- ¾ cup milk
- 2 tablespoons butter
- 3 large eggs eggs
- 1 ½ cups white sugar
- 1 ½ cups all-purpose flour
- 1 ½ teaspoons baking powder
- 1 teaspoon vanilla extract

DIRECTIONS

Step 1

Preheat oven to 350 degrees F (175 degrees C). Grease one large loaf pan or one 10 inch tube pan.

Step 2

In a saucepan over medium-low heat, combine the milk and the butter. Do not boil.

Step 3

In a large bowl beat the eggs until light colored. Gradually add the sugar to the eggs then stir in the flour and baking powder. Stir in the hot milk and butter. Beat only until combined. Stir in the vanilla. Pour the batter into the prepared pan.

Step 4

Bake at 350 degrees F (175 degrees C) for 45 to 50 minutes. Let cake cool in pan for 10 minutes. Remove cake from the pan and cool on a wire rack.

APRICOT FRUITCAKE

INGREDIENTS

- 1 cup dried apricots
- 1 cup water
- ¾ cup butter
- 1 cup white sugar
- 4 large eggs eggs
- 1 cup golden raisins
- 1 pound red and green candied cherries
- 6 piece (blank)s candied pineapple slices
- 1 pound dried mixed fruit
- 2 cups all-purpose flour, divided
- ½ teaspoon baking soda
- ½ teaspoon salt
- ½ cup apricot nectar
- 1 cup chopped walnuts

DIRECTIONS

Step 1

Preheat oven to 275 degrees F (135 degrees C). Grease two 9 inch tube pans.

Step 2

In a saucepan over medium heat cook apricots in the water until they are mushy. Press them through a sieve and let them cool.

Step 3

Separate the eggs. Beat the egg yolks until lemony colored. Then beat the egg whites until stiff peaks are formed. Set aside.

Step 4

Cream the butter or margarine and sugar together. Add the beaten egg yolks and the apricots, and mix thoroughly.

Step 5

Combine the raisins, candied cherries, candied pineapple, and mixed dried fruits in a bowl coated with one cup of the flour.

Step 6

Combine the remaining flour, baking soda, and salt. Add this flour mixture alternately to the creamed mixture with the apricot juice. Blend this batter into the mixed fruits. Add the chopped pecans or walnuts and fold in the beaten egg whites. Turn the batter into the prepared pans.

Step 7

Bake at 275 degrees F (135 degrees C) for 2 hours. Garnish cakes with candied pineapples and cherries. Makes about 24 servings.

CHRISTMAS CHERRY CAKE

INGREDIENTS

- 1 cup white sugar
- 1 cup butter
- 2 large eggs eggs
- ½ cup orange juice
- 2 cups all-purpose flour
- 1 teaspoon baking powder
- 12 ounces golden raisins
- 8 ounces halved glace cherries

DIRECTIONS

Step 1

Preheat oven to 300 degrees F (150 degrees C). Grease and line with parchment paper one 9x5 inch loaf pan.

Step 2

Cream butter or margarine and sugar together until light and fluffy. Add beaten eggs and orange juice and mix well.

Step 3

Sift flour and baking powder. Reserve 1/3 cup of flour mixture and toss with raisins and cherries (this will keep them from sinking to the bottom of the cake). Add flour mixture to batter and blend. Add floured raisins and cherries to dough and mix until just combined. Pour batter into prepared pan.

Step 4

Bake at 300 degrees F (150 degrees C) for 2-1/2 hours. Don't serve until several days old. Wrap the cake in plastic wrap or foil and store in a sealed tin.

EASY CHEWY GINGER COOKIES

INGREDIENTS

- 4 ½ cups all-purpose flour
- 4 teaspoons ground ginger
- 2 teaspoons baking powder
- 1 ½ teaspoons ground cinnamon
- ¼ teaspoon salt
- 1 ½ cups butter, softened
- 2 cups white sugar
- 2 large eggs eggs
- ½ cup molasses

- ¾ cup white sugar

DIRECTIONS

Step 1

Preheat oven to 350 degrees F (175 degrees C).

Step 2

Whisk flour, ginger, baking powder, cinnamon, and salt together in a bowl.

Step 3

Beat butter in a large bowl until creamy. Gradually beat in 2 cups sugar until light and fluffy. Add eggs, one at a time, beating well after each addition. Beat in molasses. Stir 1/2 of the flour mixture into butter mixture; add remaining flour mixture and stir until dough is just-combined.

Step 4

Pour 3/4 sugar into a shallow bowl. Roll dough into 2 inch balls and roll each ball in sugar to coat. Place sugar-coated dough balls 2 1/2-inches apart on a baking sheet.

Step 5

Bake in the preheated oven until cookies are light brown and puffed, 12 to 14 minutes. Cool on the baking sheet for 2 minutes before transferring cookies to a wire rack to cool completely.

PERFECT DOUBLE CHOCOLATE PEANUT CANDY COOKIES

INGREDIENTS

- ½ cup butter, softened
- ½ cup vegetable shortening
- ¾ cup white sugar
- ⅔ cup packed brown sugar
- 1 teaspoon vanilla extract
- 2 large eggs eggs
- ⅔ cup unsweetened cocoa powder
- 2 ¼ cups all-purpose flour
- 1 teaspoon baking soda
- ¼ teaspoon salt
- ¾ cup semi-sweet chocolate chips
- 1 ¼ cups candy-coated peanut butter pieces (such as Reese's Pieces), divided

DIRECTIONS

Step 1

Preheat oven to 350 degrees F (175 degrees C). Line baking sheets with parchment paper.

Step 2

In a large bowl, beat the butter and shortening together with an electric mixer until well combined. Beat in the white and brown sugar until the mixture is creamy, then beat the vanilla extract and eggs, followed by the cocoa powder. Beat until the mixture is even in color. In another bowl, whisk together the flour, baking soda, and salt; stir the flour mixture into the cocoa mixture until the dough is thoroughly mixed. Stir in the chocolate chips and 3/4 cup of peanut butter candies. Reserve the rest of the candy pieces.

Step 3

Cover the bowl with plastic wrap, and refrigerate the cookie dough until chilled, at least 45 minutes. Drop dough by tablespoon onto the prepared baking sheets. Gently press a few more candy pieces into the top of each cookie.

Step 4

Bake in the preheated oven 8 to 9 minutes; cool on baking sheets for 1 to 2 minutes before finishing cooling on racks.

MINI PECAN TARTS

Servings: 24 **Yield:** 4 dozen

INGREDIENTS

- ½ cup margarine
- ½ cup white sugar
- 2 large egg yolks egg yolks
- 1 teaspoon almond extract
- 2 cups sifted all-purpose flour
- ½ cup margarine
- ½ cup corn syrup
- 1 cup confectioners' sugar
- 1 cup chopped pecans

DIRECTIONS

Step 1

Preheat oven to 400 degrees F (200 degrees C).

Step 2

In a large bowl, mix 1/2 cup margarine (NOT butter) and 1/2 cup sugar. Stir in egg yolks, almond extract, and sifted flour.

Step 3

Spray tiny muffin cups with non-stick spray. Press mixture evenly into tiny muffin cups. Bake for 8 to 10 minutes.

Step 4

To make Filling: Bring to a boil 1/2 cup margarine, corn syrup, and confectioner's sugar. Stir in chopped pecans.

Step 5

Spoon into shells no more than 1/2 way. Top with pecan halves. Bake in a 350 degrees F (180 degrees C) oven for 5 minutes.

CRISP ANISE SEED BUTTER COOKIES

INGREDIENTS

- 4 cups all-purpose flour
- 1 tablespoon baking powder
- ⅛ teaspoon salt
- 1 cup butter, softened
- 1 cup white sugar
- 2 large eggs eggs
- 1 teaspoon vanilla extract
- 3 tablespoons anise seeds
- ¼ cup white sugar for decoration
- 1 teaspoon ground cinnamon

DIRECTIONS

Step 1

Sift together the flour, baking powder and salt; set aside. In a large bowl, cream together the butter and 1 cup sugar until smooth. Beat in the eggs one at a time then stir in the vanilla. Gradually mix in the sifted ingredients and anise seeds until well blended. Cover and chill for several hours or overnight.

Step 2

Preheat the oven to 400 degrees F (200 degrees C). Grease cookie sheets. On a lightly floured surface, roll the dough out to 1/4 inch in thickness. Cut into desired shapes with cookie cutters. Place cookies 1 1/2 inches apart onto cookie sheets. Sprinkle the tops with a mixture of the remaining 1/4 cup of sugar and cinnamon.

Step 3

Bake for 8 to 10 minutes in the preheated oven, until light brown. Cool on baking sheets for a few minutes before removing to wire racks to cool completely. Happy Holidays!

MARTINA COOKIES

INGREDIENTS

- 2 cups butter, softened
- 4 cups all-purpose flour
- 1 cup confectioners' sugar
- 2 teaspoons vanilla extract

DIRECTIONS

Step 1

Preheat oven to 325 degrees F (165 degrees C). Line a baking sheet with parchment paper.

Step 2

Beat butter in a large bowl until creamy and fluffy. Mix flour, confectioners' sugar, and vanilla extract into the creamed butter to form a dough. Roll dough into walnut-sized balls and arrange on the prepared baking sheet. Press the dough balls with the bottom of a glass until dough is flattened to 1/2-inch thick.

Step 3

Bake in the preheated oven until cookies are light brown, 10 to 13 minutes.

FIG FILLING FOR PASTRY

INGREDIENTS

- 1 pound dried figs
- 1 orange, zested
- ½ cup semisweet chocolate chips
- ¼ cup whiskey
- ½ cup chopped walnuts
- 1 teaspoon cinnamon
- ¼ cup maple sugar

DIRECTIONS

Step 1

Remove stems from figs with scissors. Chop in food processor in batches.

Step 2

In a non-stick pan, combine chopped figs with orange zest, chocolate chips, whiskey, walnuts, maple syrup, and cinnamon. Heat over medium heat until chocolate melts, stirring frequently. Cool completely.

WHITE CHOCOLATE AND MACADAMIA NUT COOKIES

INGREDIENTS

- 1 ¼ cups oatmeal
- ½ cup sweetened flaked coconut
- 1 cup flour
- ½ teaspoon baking powder
- ½ teaspoon baking soda
- ½ teaspoon salt
- ½ cup butter, softened
- ½ cup light brown sugar
- ½ cup white sugar
- 1 egg, at room temperature
- ½ teaspoon vanilla extract
- ½ cup white chocolate chips
- 3 ounces macadamia nuts, coarsely chopped

DIRECTIONS

Step 1

Preheat the oven to 375 degrees F (190 degrees C). Line a baking sheet with parchment paper.

Step 2

Place oatmeal in a blender and process into a fine powder. Transfer to a large bowl and set aside.

Step 3

Place coconut in the blender and process until finely chopped. Add to the bowl with the oatmeal. Add flour, baking powder, baking soda, and salt to the bowl; mix well and set aside.

Step 4

Cream butter, brown sugar, and white sugar together in a bowl. Add egg and vanilla extract. Add butter mixture to the bowl with the flour mixture and mix well. Stir in white chocolate chips and macadamia nuts.

Step 5

Roll heaping tablespoons of dough into balls and place on the prepared baking sheet.

Step 6

Bake in the preheated oven until edges start to brown lightly, 12 to 14 minutes.

ESPRESSO BISCOTTI

INGREDIENTS

- ¼ cup unsalted butter
- ¾ cup white sugar
- 3 large eggs eggs
- 1 teaspoon vanilla extract
- 3 ¼ cups pastry flour
- 1 teaspoon ground cinnamon
- 1 teaspoon baking powder
- 1 teaspoon instant espresso powder
- 2 teaspoons grated orange zest
- ½ cup chocolate chips
- ½ cup dried apricots
- ½ cup dried cranberries
- ½ cup slivered almonds
- 1 egg white, lightly beaten

DIRECTIONS

Step 1

Preheat oven to 350 degrees F (175 degrees C). Grease a cookie sheet or line it with parchment paper.

Step 2

Cream together butter and sugar in a bowl until light and fluffy. Beat in eggs and vanilla.

Step 3

Sift together the flour, cinnamon, and baking powder in a separate bowl. Mix dry ingredients into the egg mixture. Stir in the espresso powder, orange zest, chocolate chips, dried apricots, dried cranberries and almonds.

Step 4

Shape dough into two equal logs approximately 12 inches long by 2 inches diameter. Place logs on baking sheet, and flatten out to about 1 inch thickness. Brush the log with egg wash.

Step 5

Bake in the preheated oven until edges are golden and the center is firm, about 35 to 40 minutes. Remove from oven to cool on the pans. When loaves are cool enough to handle, use a serrated knife to slice the loaves diagonally into 1/2 inch thick slices. Return the slices to the baking sheet.

Step 6

Reduce oven temperature to 325 degrees F (165 degrees C). Bake until they start turning light brown, 15 to 20 minutes. Cool completely, and store in an airtight container at room temperature.

SPRINGERLE

Servings: 60 **Yield:** 10 dozen

INGREDIENTS

- 4 large eggs eggs
- 2 tablespoons butter
- 2 teaspoons baking powder
- ¼ teaspoon salt
- 2 cups white sugar
- 4 cups all-purpose flour
- ¼ cup anise seed

DIRECTIONS

Step 1

Beat eggs in large mixing bowl until very light.

Step 2

Add sugar and butter. Cream together until light and fluffy.

Step 3

Sift flour, baking powder, and salt. Add dry ingredients and combine.

Step 4

Knead dough until smooth ... add more flour to get a smooth dough if necessary.

Step 5

Cover dough and allow to chill in refrigerator for at least 2 hours.

Step 6

Roll onto slightly floured board to 1/2 inch thickness. Then roll again with springerle roller to make designs. Cut at border. Sprinkle anise seed on clean tea towel and place cookies on this. Allow to stand overnight (don't cover) to dry.

Step 7

Bake 12 to 15 minutes at 325 degrees F (170 degrees C).

Step 8

Cool completely. Store in tight tin container ... the longer they are stored, the more anise flavor they take up.

OLD FASHIONED SUGAR COOKIES IN A JAR

INGREDIENTS

- 3 cups all-purpose flour
- 1 teaspoon baking powder
- 1 teaspoon baking soda
- ⅛ teaspoon salt
- 1 ½ cups white sugar
- 1 cup butter, softened
- 2 large eggs eggs
- 1 teaspoon vanilla extract
- ½ teaspoon lemon extract

DIRECTIONS

Step 1

In a medium bowl, stir together the flour, baking powder, baking soda and salt; set aside. In a 1 quart large mouth jar, layer the sugar on the bottom and the flour mixture on top. Attach a tag with the following instructions:

Step 2

Empty the contents of the jar into a large bowl. Cut in 1 cup of softened butter until the mixture is crumbly. In a separate bowl, beat 2 eggs, 1 teaspoon vanilla and 1/2 teaspoon of lemon extract until light and fluffy. Pour into the dry ingredients and mix until well blended. Cover bowl and chill for 1 hour.

Step 3

Preheat oven to 350 degrees F (175 degrees C). On a lightly floured surface, roll the dough out to 1/4 inch in thickness. Cut into desired shapes with cookie cutters. Place cookies 1 1/2 inches apart onto cookie sheets.

Step 4

Bake for 10 to 12 minutes in the preheated oven, until edges begin to brown. You can decorate them with sugar before baking of frost after baking.

NANAIMO BARS

INGREDIENTS

- ½ cup butter
- 2 (1 ounce) squares semisweet chocolate
- ⅓ cup white sugar
- 1 ½ tablespoons pasteurized egg

- 1 cup rolled oats
- 1 ½ cups flaked coconut
- ½ cup chopped walnuts
- 1 teaspoon vanilla extract
- 2 cups confectioners' sugar
- 3 tablespoons butter, softened
- ½ teaspoon vanilla extract
- 2 ½ tablespoons milk
- 1 tablespoon butter
- 2 (1 ounce) squares semisweet chocolate

DIRECTIONS

Step 1

In a saucepan, melt 1/2 cup butter or margarine with 2 squares chocolate. Remove from the heat, and stir in white sugar, egg, rolled oats, coconut, chopped nuts, and 1 teaspoon vanilla extract. Press mixture into a greased 9 inch square pan, and chill for 1 hour.

Step 2

Combine confectioners' sugar with 3 tablespoons softened butter, 1/2 teaspoon of the vanilla, and milk. Mix until it has an icing-like consistency, and spread it over the oat mixture in the pan. Chill for 1/2 hour.

Step 3

Melt remaining 1 tablespoon butter or margarine with remaining 2 squares chocolate. Spread over the top of the bars. Chill for 4 to 5 hours.

Step 4

Cut into squares using a hot knife; dip knife in hot water, and let it melt through the chocolate.

ALMOND BUTTER COOKIES

INGREDIENTS

- Cooking spray
- ¾ cup all purpose flour
- ½ cup whole wheat pastry flour, or regular whole wheat flour
- ¾ teaspoon salt
- 1 tcaspoon baking soda
- ¼ cup unsalted butter, softened
- ¾ cup smooth, unsalted almond butter
- ⅓ cup packed light brown sugar
- ⅓ cup granulated sugar
- ½ teaspoon vanilla extract
- 1 egg
- 36 almonds raw whole almonds

DIRECTIONS

Step 1

Preheat the oven to 375 degrees. Spray two baking sheets with cooking spray. In a large bowl whisk together the flours, salt and baking soda. In another large bowl beat together the butter, almond butter and sugars until fluffy. Add the vanilla and egg and beat until well combined. Gradually stir in the flour mixture, blending well.

Step 2

Shape the dough into 3/4 inch balls, and place on the baking sheets. Place an almond in center of each cookie and press down lightly. Bake for 10-12 minutes, until lightly browned. Cool on a wire rack.

PLUM JAM COOKIES

Servings: 24 Yield: 4 dozen

INGREDIENTS

- 8 ounces butter
- 1 cup packed brown sugar
- 1 egg
- 1 teaspoon baking soda
- ¼ cup water
- 3 cups all-purpose flour
- 1 pinch salt
- 1 teaspoon baking powder
- 1 cup plum preserves

DIRECTIONS

Step 1

Preheat oven to 375 degrees F(190 degrees C).

Step 2

In a large bowl, cream together the butter and brown sugar. Beat in the egg and water. Sift together the flour, baking powder, and salt; stir into the butter mixture until well blended.

Step 3

On a lightly floured surface, roll out the dough to 1/4 inch thickness. Cut with a 2 inch round cookie cutter. Put half of the cookies onto a cookie sheet and spread 1/2 of a teaspoon of plum jam in the center of each one. With a thimble, or small cookie cutter , cut the center out of the remaining cookies. Place these on top of the jam topped cookies to make sandwiches. Press together. Bake cookies for 10 minutes then remove to a rack to cool.

EASY TOFFEE BARS

INGREDIENTS

- 1 cup butter
- 1 cup packed brown sugar
- 1 (10 ounce) package saltine crackers
- 1 (12 ounce) package semisweet chocolate chips

DIRECTIONS

Step 1

Preheat oven to 400 degrees F (200 degrees C).

Step 2

In a small saucepan over medium-high heat melt butter with brown sugar; bring to a boil and remove from heat.

Step 3

Arrange crackers (salt side up) on a jelly roll pan. Pour butter mixture over crackers.

Step 4

Bake in preheated oven for 5 minutes.

Step 5

Remove from oven and sprinkle chocolate chips over crackers. Bake for another 5 minutes.

Italian Frosted Chocolate Cookies

INGREDIENTS

- 7 cups all-purpose flour
- 2 cups white sugar
- 1 cup unsweetened cocoa powder (such as Hershey's)
- ¼ cup baking powder
- 1 ½ teaspoons ground cinnamon
- 1 ½ teaspoons ground cloves
- 1 ½ teaspoons ground allspice
- 1 teaspoon salt
- 1 large orange, zested
- ½ cup vegetable shortening (such as Crisco)
- ½ cup margarine (such as Parkay)
- 5 large eggs eggs
- 1 teaspoon vanilla extract, or to taste
- ¼ cup orange juice
- ¼ cup whole milk
- ½ (8 ounce) package cream cheese, softened
- ½ cup chopped walnuts
- 3 tablespoons whole milk, or more as needed
- 1 teaspoon orange juice, or as needed
- 3 cups confectioners' sugar, or more as needed

DIRECTIONS

Step 1

Preheat oven to 350 degrees F (175 degrees C).

Step 2

Whisk flour, white sugar, cocoa powder, baking powder, cinnamon, cloves, allspice, and salt in a large bowl. Stir orange zest into flour mixture. Mix vegetable shortening and margarine into dry ingredients, using your hands, until mixture is crumbly.

Step 3

Beat eggs and vanilla extract in a bowl with an electric mixer until foamy; add egg mixture, 1/4 cup orange juice, and 1/4 cup milk to flour mixture and knead dough in the bowl until thoroughly combined and dough doesn't stick to your hands, about 8 minutes. Dough will be stiff. Knead cream cheese thoroughly into dough, followed by walnuts.

Step 4

Form dough into balls about 1 1/2 inches in diameter and place onto ungreased baking sheets.

Step 5

Bake cookies in the preheated oven until lightly browned, 12 to 14 minutes. Cool cookies on racks.

Step 6

Beat 3 tablespoons milk, 1 teaspoon orange juice, and 1 cup confectioners' sugar in a bowl until smooth; gradually beat in remaining confectioners' sugar until frosting is thick and drizzles slowly from a spoon.

Step 7

Dip tops of cookies into frosting and place frosted cookies on racks with waxed paper underneath to catch drips. Let cookies dry overnight.

CHERRY SHORTBREAD COOKIES

Servings: 12 **Yield:** 2 dozen

INGREDIENTS

- 1 cup all-purpose flour
- ½ cup confectioners' sugar
- ½ cup cornstarch
- ½ cup chopped cherries
- 1 cup butter

DIRECTIONS

Step 1

Preheat oven to 300 degrees F (150 degrees C).

Step 2

Cream butter and confectioners' sugar together. Add the cornstarch and flour and mix well. Stir in the chopped cherries. Drop teaspoonfuls of the dough onto a cookie sheet then press with tines of a floured fork.

Step 3

Bake at 300 degrees F (150 degrees C) until lightly golden, about 10 to 15 minutes.

STRAWBERRY PRESERVES-FILLED

COOKIES

INGREDIENTS

- 1 cup shortening
- 1 cup white sugar
- 1 cup brown sugar
- ¼ cup milk
- 1 teaspoon vinegar
- 2 large eggs eggs
- 1 teaspoon vanilla extract
- 3 ½ cups all-purpose flour
- 1 teaspoon baking powder
- 1 teaspoon baking soda
- 1 teaspoon salt
- 1 teaspoon ground nutmeg
- 6 tablespoons strawberry preserves, or as needed

DIRECTIONS

Step 1

Beat shortening, white sugar, and brown sugar in a bowl using an electric mixer until creamy and smooth.

Step 2

Mix milk and vinegar together and let stand 5 minutes to make 'sour milk'. Stir sour milk, eggs, and vanilla extract into shortening mixture.

Step 3

Sift flour, baking powder, baking soda, salt, and nutmeg together in a large bowl. Mix flour mixture into shortening mixture until incorporated. Refrigerate until fully chilled, 2 hours to overnight.

Step 4

Preheat oven to 350 degrees F (175 degrees C).

Step 5

Roll dough to a 1/8-inch thickness on a floured surface; cut into 2-inch rounds using a cookie cutter. Spoon 1 teaspoon preserves into the center of half the cookies; cover with remaining cookies. Lightly press edges of cookies together using a fork. Cut criss-cross slits into the top of each cookie using a knife. Arrange cookies on an ungreased baking sheet.

Step 6

Bake in the preheated oven until cookies are golden, 13 to 15 minutes.

REINDEER COOKIES

INGREDIENTS

- 1 cup butter, softened
- 1 cup white sugar

- 1 cup smooth peanut butter
- 2 large eggs eggs
- 1 teaspoon vanilla extract
- ½ teaspoon salt
- 3 cups all-purpose flour
- 2 teaspoons baking soda
- 72 eaches small pretzel twists, or as needed
- ½ cup chocolate chips, or as needed

DIRECTIONS

Step 1

Preheat oven to 375 degrees F (190 degrees C).

Step 2

Beat butter, sugar, peanut butter, eggs, vanilla extract, and salt together in a bowl until smooth and creamy. Stir flour and baking soda into creamed butter mixture until well incorporated.

Step 3

Roll dough into 36 balls. Flatten each ball and shape into an upside-down triangle. Press two pretzels into the two top corners of each triangle for the antlers. Press two chocolate chips into the center of each triangle for the eyes, and one chocolate chip or M&M on the bottom of the triangle for the nose. Arrange cookies on baking sheets.

Step 4

Bake in the preheated oven until cookies are golden brown, 10 to 15 minutes.

GRANDMA'S CORN FLAKE COCONUT MACAROONS

INGREDIENTS

- 1 egg white
- ½ cup white sugar
- ¼ teaspoon salt
- ½ teaspoon vanilla extract
- ½ cup shredded coconut
- 1 cup cornflakes cereal

DIRECTIONS

Step 1

Preheat oven to 300 degrees F (150 degrees C).

Step 2

Grease a baking sheet.

Step 3

Beat egg white in a bowl with an electric hand-mixer until stiff peaks form.

Step 4

Gradually beat sugar, 1 tablespoon at a time, into egg whites until fully incorporated. Stir salt and vanilla extract into egg whites until thoroughly mixed.

Step 5

Fold coconut and corn flakes into the mixture.

Step 6

Drop coconut mixture by the teaspoon onto the prepared baking sheet.

Step 7

Bake cookies in the preheated oven until lightly crisp, 20 minutes.

Step 8

Transfer cookies to wire rack to cool, at least 15 minutes.

EGGNOG COOKIES

INGREDIENTS

- 1 cup butter, softened
- 2 cups white sugar
- 1 teaspoon vanilla extract
- 4 large eggs eggs
- 3 cups all-purpose flour
- 2 teaspoons baking powder
- ½ teaspoon salt
- ½ teaspoon ground nutmeg

DIRECTIONS

Step 1

In a medium bowl, cream together the butter, sugar, and vanilla. Beat in eggs, one at a time. Sift together the flour, baking powder, salt and nutmeg; gradually stir into creamed mixture. Cover and refrigerate until firm.

Step 2

Preheat oven to 375 degrees F (190 degrees C).

Step 3

Drop by heaping spoonfuls onto an unprepared cookie sheet. Bake for 6 to 8 minutes in the preheated oven. Cookies should be lightly browned.

SNOW FLAKES

INGREDIENTS

- 1 cup butter flavored shortening
- 1 (3 ounce) package cream cheese, softened
- 1 cup white sugar

- 1 egg yolk
- 1 teaspoon vanilla extract
- 1 teaspoon orange zest
- 2 ½ cups all-purpose flour
- ½ teaspoon salt
- ¼ teaspoon ground cinnamon

DIRECTIONS

Step 1

Preheat oven to 350 degrees F (175 degrees C).

Step 2

In a medium bowl, cream together shortening, cream cheese, and sugar. Beat in egg yolk, vanilla, and orange zest. Continue beating until light and fluffy. Gradually stir in flour, salt, and cinnamon. Fill the cookie press, and form cookies on ungreased cookie sheet.

Step 3

Bake in preheated oven for 10 to 12 minutes. Remove from cookie sheet, and cool on wire racks.

OATMEAL THUMBPRINTS

Servings: 30 **Yield:** 5 dozen

INGREDIENTS

- ½ cup butter, softened
- ½ cup shortening
- 1 cup packed brown sugar
- ¾ cup white sugar
- 2 large eggs eggs
- 2 ½ cups all-purpose flour
- 1 teaspoon baking soda
- 1 teaspoon salt
- ½ teaspoon ground cinnamon
- ½ cup water
- 2 ½ cups quick cooking oats
- ½ cup finely chopped walnuts
- 1 teaspoon almond extract
- ¼ cup raspberry jam

DIRECTIONS

Step 1

Preheat oven to 400 degrees F (205 degrees C).

Step 2

Cream butter and shortening with sugars. Beat in eggs. In a separate bowl, sift together flour, baking soda, salt, nuts and cinnamon. Add to butter mixture alternately with water. Stir in oats and almond extract.

Step 3

Drop by teaspoons on ungreased cookie sheets. Make a small indentation in each cookie. Fill with preserves.

Step 4

Bake for 10-12 minutes.

PISTACHIO CREAM CHEESE FINGERS

INGREDIENTS

- 1 cup butter, softened
- 1 cup white sugar
- 1 (8 ounce) package cream cheese, softened
- 1 egg
- 1 teaspoon vanilla extract
- 2 ¼ cups all-purpose flour
- 1 (3 ounce) package instant pistachio pudding mix
- 1 teaspoon baking powder
- ½ teaspoon salt
- 3 (1 ounce) squares semisweet chocolate
- 1 teaspoon shortening

DIRECTIONS

Step 1

In a large bowl, cream together the butter, sugar, and cream cheese until light and fluffy. Beat in the egg and vanilla. Combine the flour, dry pudding mix, baking powder, and salt; stir into the creamed mixture. Cover dough, and refrigerate for at least one hour for easier handling.

Step 2

Preheat oven to 350 degrees F (175 degrees C). Grease cookie sheets. Shape teaspoonfuls of dough into finger shapes, about 1 1/2 inches long. Place cookies on prepared cookie sheets.

Step 3

Bake for 9 to 12 minutes in the preheated oven, or until set and very lightly browned on bottoms. Cool completely on a wire rack.

Step 4

In small saucepan over low heat, melt together chocolate and shortening, stirring constantly until smooth and well blended. Drizzle a small amount of chocolate over each cookie. Allow the chocolate to set before storing.

MORAVIAN GINGER COOKIES

Servings: 30 **Yield:** 5 dozen

INGREDIENTS

- 3 tablespoons shortening

- 2 tablespoons brown sugar
- ⅓ cup molasses
- 1 ¼ cups all-purpose flour
- ¼ teaspoon baking soda
- ½ teaspoon salt
- ¼ teaspoon ground cinnamon
- ¼ teaspoon ground ginger
- ¼ teaspoon ground cloves
- 1 pinch ground nutmeg
- 1 dash ground allspice

DIRECTIONS

Step 1

In a medium bowl, cream together the shortening, brown sugar and molasses until smooth. Sift together the flour, baking soda, salt, cinnamon, ginger, cloves, nutmeg and allspice; blend into the creamed mixture. Work dough with hands until well blended. Cover and chill for about 4 hours. Dough must be thoroughly chilled to hold together.

Step 2

Preheat oven to 375 degrees F (190 degrees C). Roll out dough paper thin a little at a time. Cut into desired shapes using cookie cutters. Place on greased baking sheets.

Step 3

Bake 5 to 6 minutes in the preheated oven, or until lightly browned.

ROSEMARY SLICES

INGREDIENTS

- ½ cup butter, softened
- ¾ cup white sugar
- 1 medium egg
- 1 cup whole wheat flour
- ¾ cup all-purpose flour
- 1 tablespoon finely chopped fresh rosemary
- ½ teaspoon baking powder

DIRECTIONS

Step 1

Beat the butter and sugar together in a bowl until creamy and smooth, and stir in the egg until well incorporated. Stir in the whole wheat flour, all-purpose flour, rosemary, and baking powder until well blended. Cut the dough into 2 equal-sized pieces, and shape each piece into a log about 1 1/4-inch in diameter. Wrap the logs in plastic wrap, and refrigerate at least 2 hours, or place in freezer for about 1 hour.

Step 2

Preheat an oven to 350 degrees F (175 degrees C). Line baking sheets with parchment paper.

Step 3

Cut the logs of dough into thin slices, 1/8 to 1/4-inch thick. Place the slices on the prepared baking sheets, and bake in the preheated oven until the cookies are set and the edges turn golden brown, 10 to 12 minutes. Cool for 1 minute on baking sheets before removing to wire racks to finish cooling.

Kourambiedes

Servings: 18 **Yield:** 3 dozen

INGREDIENTS

- 1 cup unsalted butter
- 4 tablespoons confectioners' sugar
- 1 teaspoon vanilla extract
- 2 cups sifted all-purpose flour
- 1 cup chopped pecans
- 36 eaches whole cloves
- ½ cup confectioners' sugar

DIRECTIONS

Step 1

Preheat oven to 350 degrees F (175 degrees C).

Step 2

In a medium bowl, cream the butter and confectioners' sugar together. Stir in the vanilla, then the flour, then the pecans.

Step 3

Roll dough into walnut sized balls and insert a clove into each one. Place on an unprepared cookie sheet and bake for 15 to 18 minutes in the preheated oven. Roll the cookies in powdered sugar while they are still hot. Remove cloves before serving or warn guests to remove them.

GREAT GRANDAD'S SUGAR COOKIES

INGREDIENTS

- 6 cups all-purpose flour
- 1 tablespoon baking powder
- 1 teaspoon ground nutmeg
- 1 pinch salt
- 2 ½ cups white sugar
- 1 ½ cups shortening
- 1 teaspoon baking soda
- 1 cup sour milk
- 3 large eggs eggs, beaten
- 1 teaspoon vanilla extract

DIRECTIONS

Step 1

Preheat oven to 350 degrees F (175 degrees C). Line cookie sheets with parchment paper.

Step 2

In a medium bowl, stir together 4 cups flour, baking powder, nutmeg, salt, and sugar. Cut in the shortening until the mixture resembles coarse crumbs. Stir in baking soda, sour milk, beaten eggs, and vanilla. Stir as little as possible, and add the remaining flour as necessary to make dough thick enough to roll out.

Step 3

On a lightly floured surface, roll out dough 1/4 inch thick. Cut into desired shapes with cookie cutters. Place cookies 1 inch apart on the prepared cookie sheets.

Step 4

Bake for 8 to 10 minutes in preheated oven. Cool on baking sheets.

GERMAN OATMEAL DATE COOKIES

INGREDIENTS

- 10 tablespoons unsalted butter, divided
- 3 cups rolled oats
- 2 large eggs eggs
- ½ cup white sugar
- 1 teaspoon vanilla sugar
- 1 teaspoon baking powder
- 1 ½ cups finely chopped, pitted dates

DIRECTIONS

Step 1

Melt 9 tablespoons butter in a small saucepan over low heat; mix in oats. Remove from heat and let cool, about 20 minutes.

Step 2

Mix eggs, sugar, vanilla sugar, and baking powder together in a large bowl; stir in dates-oat mixture.

Step 3

Preheat oven to 350 degrees F (175 degrees C). Grease a baking sheet with remaining 1 tablespoon butter.

Step 4

Use 2 teaspoons to place little mounds of oat-date mixture 2 inches apart onto the baking sheets.

Step 5

Bake in the preheated oven until lightly browned on the top and bottom, about 20 minutes.

RICCIARELLI

INGREDIENTS

- 2 ¼ cups white sugar
- 2 cups blanched almonds
- ½ cup egg whites
- 1 drop vanilla extract
- ¼ cup confectioners' sugar, or as needed
- 2 tablespoons all-purpose flour

DIRECTIONS

Step 1

Combine white sugar and almonds in the bowl of a food processor; pulse into a fine powder. Pour into a bowl.

Step 2

Combine 1/4 cup egg whites and vanilla extract in a bowl; add to almond-sugar mixture, mixing as little as possible. Wrap dough in plastic wrap and refrigerate for 12 hours.

Step 3

Line a baking sheet with parchment paper.

Step 4

Remove dough from fridge. Sift 2 tablespoons confectioners' sugar and flour onto a clean work surface. Place dough in the center and add remaining 1/4 cup egg whites. Knead egg whites into dough until soft and smooth, adding additional confectioners' sugar and flour as needed.

Step 5

Roll portions of dough into 1-inch-thick logs. Take walnut-sized dough pieces from each log and shape into diamonds with slightly wet hands. Place cookies on the prepared baking sheet and generously dust with confectioner's sugar. Let rest at room temperature for 1 to 2 hours.

Step 6

Preheat oven to 350 degrees F (175 degrees C).

Step 7

Bake cookies in the preheated oven until lightly golden, 7 to 8 minutes. Cool on the baking sheet before serving.

PEANUT BUTTER DREAMS

INGREDIENTS

- ½ cup butter
- 4 cups confectioners' sugar
- 2 cups creamy peanut butter
- 3 cups crisp rice cereal
- 2 cups semisweet chocolate chips
- 4 tablespoons shortening

DIRECTIONS

Step 1

In a large mixing bowl, mix butter, sugar, peanut butter and crisp rice cereal together thoroughly.

Step 2

Roll into small balls and set aside.

Step 3

Melt chocolate chips and shortening in a small saucepan over low heat. Remove from heat. Coat the small balls in the chocolate mixture. Refrigerate for several hours.

POLISH CHRISTMAS COOKIES

INGREDIENTS

- 1 cup butter
- 1 cup shortening
- 2 cups white sugar
- 5 large eggs eggs
- 7 ½ cups all-purpose flour
- 6 teaspoons baking powder
- ½ teaspoon salt
- ½ ounce anise extract

DIRECTIONS

Step 1

Preheat oven to 350 degrees F (175 degrees C).

Step 2

Cream the butter, shortening and the sugar together. Stir in the eggs and continue to beat. Add the anise flavoring. Stir in 7 cups of the flour, the baking powder and the salt. Mix until the dough is soft. Add the additional cup of flour if needed. Chill the dough.

Step 3

On a lightly floured surface roll out the dough and cut with cookie cutters. Place cookies on greased cookie sheets.

Step 4

Bake at 350 degrees F (175 degrees C) for 12 to 15 minutes. Frost and decorate when cookies are cooled.

CHOCOLATE CHIP COOKIES WITH PEPPERMINT EXTRACT

INGREDIENTS

- 1 cup unsalted butter, softened
- 1 cup white sugar
- 1 cup packed light brown sugar

- 2 large eggs eggs
- 2 teaspoons vanilla extract
- 1 teaspoon peppermint extract
- 1 teaspoon baking soda
- 2 teaspoons hot water
- 3 cups all-purpose flour
- 1 teaspoon salt
- ½ teaspoon cream of tartar
- 2 cups semisweet chocolate chips
- 10 drops green food coloring, or more to taste

DIRECTIONS

Step 1

Preheat oven to 350 degrees F (175 degrees C).

Step 2

Combine butter, white sugar, and brown sugar in a large bowl; beat with an electric mixer until creamy. Beat in eggs. Stir in vanilla extract and peppermint extract. Dissolve baking soda in hot water and mix into the batter.

Step 3

Combine flour, salt, and cream of tartar in a separate bowl. Add to the batter gradually; mix well. Stir in chocolate chips.

Step 4

Drop spoonfuls of batter onto ungreased baking sheets.

Step 5

Bake in the preheated oven until edges are nicely browned, about 10 minutes. Cool on the baking sheets for 1 minute; transfer to a wire rack to cool completely.

CHOCOLATE ORANGE COOKIES

INGREDIENTS

- 1 (1 ounce) square unsweetened chocolate
- ¾ cup butter
- ¾ cup white sugar
- 1 egg
- 1 teaspoon vanilla extract
- 1 ½ cups all-purpose flour
- 1 teaspoon baking powder
- 1 pinch salt
- 1 tablespoon orange zest

DIRECTIONS

Step 1

Preheat the oven to 350 degrees F (175 degrees C). In a microwave-safe dish, melt the unsweetened chocolate, stirring frequently until smooth. Set aside.

Step 2

In a medium bowl, cream together the butter and sugar until smooth. Beat in the egg and vanilla. Combine the flour, baking powder, and salt; stir into the creamed mixture. Divide dough in two. Mix orange zest into one half, and melted chocolate into the other half. Use a bit of each mixture to form a ball about 1 inch in diameter.

Step 3

Bake for 8 to 10 minutes in the preheated oven, or until center is set. Cool on wire racks.

GRANDMA'S MOLASSES GINGER COOKIES

INGREDIENTS

- 1 ½ cups sugar, plus more for sprinkling
- 2 sticks butter, softened
- ¾ cup Grandma's Original Molasses
- 1 egg
- 1 teaspoon Spice Islands Pure Vanilla Extract
- 3 cups flour, plus more for dusting
- 1 teaspoon Clabber Girl Baking Soda
- 1 teaspoon Clabber Girl Baking Powder
- 1 teaspoon Spice Islands Ground Nutmeg
- 1 teaspoon Spice Islands Ground Cloves
- 1 tablespoon Spice Islands Ground Ginger
- 1 tablespoon Spice Islands Ground Saigon Cinnamon

DIRECTIONS

Step 1

In a large bowl, whip together sugar, butter, molasses, egg, and vanilla. Mix in flour, baking soda, baking powder, and spices until dough comes together. Wrap well and refrigerate overnight.

Step 2

Preheat the oven to 350 degrees F.

Step 3

Roll cookie dough into 1-inch balls and roll in sugar to coat. Arrange on rimmed baking sheets. Bake for 15 minutes.

Cook's Note:

Substitute margarine for butter, if desired.

NO-BAKE HAYSTACKS

INGREDIENTS

- 3 cups quick cooking oats
- 1 cup flaked coconut
- 1 cup roasted peanuts, chopped
- 1 cup raisins
- 2 cups white sugar
- ½ cup milk
- ¼ cup butter
- ¼ cup unsweetened cocoa powder
- 1 teaspoon vanilla

DIRECTIONS

Step 1

Mix the oats, coconut, peanuts, and raisins together in a large bowl.

Step 2

Stir the sugar, milk, butter, and cocoa powder together in a saucepan and bring to a boil; boil for 1 minute and immediately remove from heat. Stir the vanilla into the cocoa mixture; pour over the oat mixture and stir to coat. Scoop heaping tablespoonfuls of the mixture and drop into haystack-like piles onto waxed paper; allow to cool completely before serving.

SUPER DUPER CHOCOLATE COOKIES

INGREDIENTS

- 4 (1 ounce) squares unsweetened chocolate
- ½ cup vegetable shortening
- 2 cups white sugar
- 2 teaspoons vanilla extract
- 4 large eggs eggs
- 2 cups all-purpose flour
- 2 teaspoons baking powder
- ⅛ teaspoon salt
- ½ cup chopped walnuts
- ¾ cup confectioners' sugar

DIRECTIONS

Step 1

Melt the chocolate and shortening in a saucepan over low heat. Remove from heat and mix in sugar and vanilla. Beat in eggs 1 at a time. In a bowl, sift together flour, baking powder and salt. Stir in the chocolate mixture and nuts. Chill dough in the refrigerator 3 hours or overnight.

Step 2

Preheat oven to 350 degrees F (175 degrees C). Grease cookie sheets.

Step 3

Place confectioners' sugar in a bowl. Roll dough into 1 inch balls. Roll dough balls in confectioners' sugar to coat. Arrange 3 inches apart on the prepared cookie sheets.

Step 4

Bake 12 to 15 minutes in the preheated oven. The cookies will look soft when removed from the oven. Transfer to a wire rack to cool. Enjoy!

CRANBERRY-ORANGE SHORTBREAD COOKIES WITH APRICOTS

INGREDIENTS

- 1 ¾ cups all-purpose flour
- ¼ teaspoon baking powder
- ¼ teaspoon salt
- ¼ teaspoon ground nutmeg
- 1 cup unsalted butter, softened
- ½ cup white sugar
- 1 teaspoon vanilla extract
- 2 large oranges, zested
- 1 cup finely chopped dried cranberries
- ½ cup finely chopped dried apricots

DIRECTIONS

Step 1

Combine flour, baking powder, salt, and nutmeg in a bowl; mix together.

Step 2

Cream butter in a large bowl using an electric blender until fluffy and lightened in color slightly. Add sugar and cream on medium-high speed until light and fluffy, several more minutes. Mix in vanilla and orange zest. Add flour mixture in 3 batches and mix until just combined, kneading the last addition by hand. Knead in cranberries and apricots.

Step 3

Divide dough in half and roll out into two 1 1/2x7-inch long logs. Wrap each log in parchment paper and refrigerate until dough is chilled, at least 4 hours.

Step 4

Preheat the oven to 350 degrees F (175 degrees C). Line 2 baking sheets with parchment paper.

Step 5

Remove dough from the refrigerator and cut each log into about 16 slices that are 1/3-inch thick. Place slices 1 inch apart on prepared baking sheets.

Step 6

Bake in the preheated oven until cookies just begin to turn slightly golden on bottom, 20 to 25 minutes. Cool on baking sheets for 5 minutes before removing to wire racks to cool completely. Store in an airtight container.

CHOCOLATE SPRITZ (COOKIE PRESS)

INGREDIENTS

- 1 ½ cups butter, softened
- 1 cup white sugar
- ¼ cup unsweetened cocoa powder
- 1 teaspoon baking powder
- 1 egg
- 1 teaspoon vanilla extract
- 3 ¼ cups all-purpose flour

DIRECTIONS

Step 1

Preheat oven to 375 degrees F (190 degrees C).

Step 2

Beat butter in a large mixing bowl using an electric mixer until creamy; add sugar, cocoa powder, and baking powder. Beat until combined. Scrape sides of bowl down if needed. Stir egg and vanilla extract into butter mixture until just combined; mix in flour.

Step 3

Fill the cookie press with dough; press cookies onto an ungreased baking sheet.

Step 4

Bake in the preheated oven until edges of cookies are lightly browned, 8 to 10 minutes.

ORANGE MELTAWAY COOKIES

INGREDIENTS

- 2 cups all-purpose flour
- 1 teaspoon baking soda
- 1 teaspoon cream of tartar
- 1 cup butter
- 1 ½ cups sifted confectioners' sugar
- 1 teaspoon orange extract
- 1 tablespoon grated orange zest
- 1 beaten egg
- ½ cup confectioners' sugar, for dusting

DIRECTIONS

Step 1

Preheat oven to 375 degrees F (190 degrees C). Line baking sheets with parchment paper, and set aside.

Step 2

Mix the flour, baking soda, and cream of tartar in a bowl. In another bowl, beat the butter and 1 1/2 cups confectioners' sugar together with an electric mixer until light and fluffy. Mix in orange extract, grated orange zest, and egg. Stir in the flour mixture, and blend well.

Step 3

Drop teaspoon-sized portions of dough about 2 inches apart onto the parchment lined baking sheets. The cookies will spread out to about 1 1/2 inches when baked.

Step 4

Bake in the preheated oven for 10 to 14 minutes, until the cookies are light brown. Remove from the oven, and sift remaining confectioners' sugar onto the hot cookies. Allow to cool, and store in an airtight container.

SNOWBALLS

INGREDIENTS

- 1 cup 2% milk
- 1 cup white sugar
- ¼ cup butter
- ¼ cup unsweetened cocoa powder
- 2 teaspoons vanilla extract
- 2 cups rolled oats
- 2 ½ cups unsweetened shredded coconut, divided

DIRECTIONS

Step 1

Combine milk, sugar, butter, and cocoa powder in a large pot; bring to a boil for 3 minutes. Stir vanilla extract into the milk mixture; boil another 2 minutes. Remove pot from heat.

Step 2

Stir oats and 2 cups coconut into the milk mixture until thoroughly mixed; cool for 5 minutes.

Step 3

Spread 1/2 cup coconut onto a plate. Roll the mixture into 24 balls and roll in the coconut. Set on a sheet of parchment paper until finished.

MOM'S PEANUT BUTTER BLOSSOM COOKIES

INGREDIENTS

- ¾ cup peanut butter
- ½ cup shortening
- ⅓ cup white sugar
- ⅓ cup light brown sugar
- 1 egg
- 2 tablespoons milk
- 1 teaspoon vanilla extract
- 1 ½ cups all-purpose flour

- 1 teaspoon baking soda
- ½ teaspoon salt
- 1 (8 ounce) package milk chocolate candy kisses (such as Hershey's Kisses®), unwrapped

DIRECTIONS

Step 1

Preheat oven to 375 degrees F (190 degrees C).

Step 2

Beat peanut butter and shortening together in a bowl using an electric mixer until smooth and creamy; add white sugar and brown sugar and beat until fluffy. Add egg, milk, and vanilla extract to creamed mixture and beat until smooth.

Step 3

Mix flour, baking soda, and salt together in a separate bowl; gradually beat into the creamed mixture until dough is just mixed. Shape dough into 1-inch balls and arrange on a baking sheet.

Step 4

Bake in the preheated oven until cookies are lightly browned, 8 to 10 minutes. Immediately press a chocolate kiss into the center of each cookie. Transfer cookies to a wire rack to cool.

CHOCOLATE SPRITZ (COOKIE PRESS)

INGREDIENTS

- 1 ½ cups butter, softened
- 1 cup white sugar
- ¼ cup unsweetened cocoa powder
- 1 teaspoon baking powder
- 1 egg
- 1 teaspoon vanilla extract
- 3 ¼ cups all-purpose flour

DIRECTIONS

Step 1

Preheat oven to 375 degrees F (190 degrees C).

Step 2

Beat butter in a large mixing bowl using an electric mixer until creamy; add sugar, cocoa powder, and baking powder. Beat until combined. Scrape sides of bowl down if needed. Stir egg and vanilla extract into butter mixture until just combined; mix in flour.

Step 3

Fill the cookie press with dough; press cookies onto an ungreased baking sheet.

Step 4

Bake in the preheated oven until edges of cookies are lightly browned, 8 to 10 minutes.

RICCIARELLI

INGREDIENTS

- 2 ¼ cups white sugar
- 2 cups blanched almonds
- ½ cup egg whites
- 1 drop vanilla extract
- ¼ cup confectioners' sugar, or as needed
- 2 tablespoons all-purpose flour

DIRECTIONS

Step 1

Combine white sugar and almonds in the bowl of a food processor; pulse into a fine powder. Pour into a bowl.

Step 2

Combine 1/4 cup egg whites and vanilla extract in a bowl; add to almond-sugar mixture, mixing as little as possible. Wrap dough in plastic wrap and refrigerate for 12 hours.

Step 3

Line a baking sheet with parchment paper.

Step 4

Remove dough from fridge. Sift 2 tablespoons confectioners' sugar and flour onto a clean work surface. Place dough in the center and add remaining 1/4 cup egg whites. Knead egg whites into dough until soft and smooth, adding additional confectioners' sugar and flour as needed.

Step 5

Roll portions of dough into 1-inch-thick logs. Take walnut-sized dough pieces from each log and shape into diamonds with slightly wet hands. Place cookies on the prepared baking sheet and generously dust with confectioner's sugar. Let rest at room temperature for 1 to 2 hours.

Step 6

Preheat oven to 350 degrees F (175 degrees C).

Step 7

Bake cookies in the preheated oven until lightly golden, 7 to 8 minutes. Cool on the baking sheet before serving.

LEBKUCHEN

Servings: 84 **Yield:** 14 dozen

INGREDIENTS

- 3 cups honey
- 2 ¼ cups packed brown sugar
- 3 large eggs eggs

- 1 tablespoon lemon zest
- 3 tablespoons lemon juice
- 8 ¼ cups all-purpose flour
- 1 ½ teaspoons baking soda
- 1 tablespoon ground cinnamon
- 1 ½ teaspoons ground allspice
- 1 ½ teaspoons ground nutmeg
- 1 teaspoon ground cloves
- 1 cup chopped candied citron
- 1 cup chopped pecans
- 2 cups sliced almonds
- 1 ½ cups white sugar
- ¾ cup water
- ⅓ cup sifted confectioners' sugar

DIRECTIONS

Step 1

Bring honey to a boil in a large Dutch oven; remove from heat, and cool slightly. Stir in brown sugar, beaten eggs, lemon rind, and juice.

Step 2

Combine flour, baking soda, and spices in a large mixing bowl; gradually add to honey mixture, stirring well. Stir in citron and chopped pecans, blending well. Cover and chill overnight.

Step 3

Preheat oven to 400 degrees F (200 degrees C).

Step 4

Shape dough into 1-inch balls; place 2 inches apart on greased cookie sheets. Gently press ball to 1/4-inch thickness with bottom of a glass dipped in cool water. Gently press an almond slice in the center of each cookie. Bake for about 10 minutes. Remove cookie sheets from oven. Brush glaze over cookies and remove to wire racks to cool.

Step 5

To Make Glaze: Combine 1 1/2 cups sugar and water in a small heavy saucepan; cook over low heat, stirring until sugar dissolves. Cook over high heat, without stirring, until mixture reaches thread stage (230 degrees F). Remove from heat; stir in confectioners' sugar, mixing well. Place over low heat, if necessary, to maintain basting consistency.

SPRINGERLE

INGREDIENTS

- 4 large eggs eggs
- 1 pound confectioners' sugar
- 2 teaspoons anise extract
- 4 ¼ cups sifted all-purpose flour
- 2 teaspoons baking powder

DIRECTIONS

Step 1

In a large bowl, beat eggs until light with an electric mixer on high speed. Reduce speed and add the anise extract and confectioners' sugar. Continue beating at medium speed until well combined. Sift together the flour and baking powder; stir into the egg mixture, dough will be quite stiff.

Step 2

Roll out dough to 3/8 inch thickness. Imprint with a springerle board and cut apart. Place cookies onto a cookie sheet and let rest uncovered overnight.

Step 3

Preheat oven to 350 degrees F (175 degrees C). Bake cookies for 7 to 10 minutes.

WHITE CHOCOLATE THUMBPRINT COOKIES

INGREDIENTS

- 1 pound butter, softened
- 1 ½ cups white sugar
- 1 teaspoon vanilla extract
- 4 cups all-purpose flour
- 2 teaspoons baking powder
- 1 cup chopped walnuts
- 1 (8 ounce) jar seedless raspberry jam
- 3 (1.55 ounce) bars white chocolate, chopped
- 1 tablespoon vegetable shortening

DIRECTIONS

Step 1

Beat butter, sugar, and vanilla extract together in a bowl until creamy and smooth. Mix flour and baking powder together in a separate bowl; gradually beat flour mixture into creamed butter mixture until dough is smooth. Fold walnuts into the dough. Refrigerate dough for 1 hour.

Step 2

Preheat oven to 325 degrees F (165 degrees C).

Step 3

Roll cookie dough into 6 dozen small balls and place them 2 inches apart on a baking sheet. Press the center of each ball using your thumb to form a small well. Fill the depressions with jam.

Step 4

Bake in the preheated oven until cookies are light golden brown, about 18 minutes.

Step 5

Melt white chocolate and shortening together in the top of a double boiler over simmering water, stirring frequently and scraping down the sides with a rubber spatula to avoid scorching. Drizzle melted white chocolate mixture over cookies.

Step 6

Cool cookies on the sheet for 5 minutes before removing to cool completely on a wire rack.

MOM'S SUGAR COOKIES

INGREDIENTS

- 1 cup butter, softened
- 1 egg
- 1 teaspoon pure vanilla extract
- ½ teaspoon almond extract
- 1 ½ cups confectioners' sugar
- 2 ½ cups all-purpose flour
- 1 teaspoon baking soda
- 1 teaspoon cream of tartar

DIRECTIONS

Step 1

Beat butter, egg, vanilla extract, and almond extract together in a bowl using an electric mixer until smooth. Add confectioners' sugar and beat until incorporated. Mix flour, baking soda, and cream of tartar into butter mixture until dough sticks together. Cover bowl with plastic wrap and refrigerate for at least 3 hours.

Step 2

Preheat oven to 375 degrees F (190 degrees C). Lightly grease baking sheets.

Step 3

Cut dough into quarters and roll each quarter onto a floured work surface to almost 1/4-inch thickness. Cut dough into shapes using cookie cutters and arrange on the prepared baking sheets.

Step 4

Bake each batch in the preheated oven until edges start to brown, about 8 minutes.

GINGERBREAD MAN COOKIES

INGREDIENTS

- 3 ½ cups all-purpose flour
- 1 ½ teaspoons ground ginger
- 1 ½ teaspoons ground cinnamon
- ¼ teaspoon salt
- ½ cup shortening
- ½ cup white sugar
- 1 egg
- 1 cup molasses
- 1 teaspoon baking soda
- 1 ½ teaspoons warm water

- ¼ cup raisins for decorating

DIRECTIONS

Step 1

Combine flour, ginger, cinnamon, and salt in a bowl and set aside.

Step 2

In large bowl, cream shortening and sugar until smooth. Mix in egg and molasses. Dissolve baking soda in 1 1/2 teaspoons warm water and add to egg mixture; stir until combined.

Step 3

Mix in dry ingredients well blended. Shape dough into a disk, wrap in plastic, and refrigerate overnight.

Step 4

Preheat oven to 350 degrees F. Grease cookie sheets or line them with parchment paper.

Step 5

Lightly flour a work surface. Roll out dough to a thickness of 1/4 inch. Cut out gingerbread men using cookie cutters and place 2 inches apart on cookie sheets. Use raisins to make eyes, noses and buttons.

Step 6

Bake in the preheated oven, or until firm, 10 to 12 minutes. Let cool on wire racks.

CHOCOLATE COVERED ORANGE BALLS

INGREDIENTS

- 1 pound confectioners' sugar
- 1 (12 ounce) package vanilla wafers, crushed
- 1 cup chopped walnuts
- ¼ pound butter
- 1 (6 ounce) can frozen orange juice concentrate, thawed
- 1 ½ pounds milk chocolate, melted

DIRECTIONS

Step 1

In a large bowl, combine the confectioners sugar, vanilla wafers, walnuts, butter and orange juice. Mix well and shape into 1 inch round balls; allow to dry for 1 hour.

Step 2

Place chocolate chips in top of double boiler. Stir frequently over medium heat until melted.

Step 3

Dip balls into melted chocolate and place in decorative paper cups.

RUM SUGAR COOKIES

INGREDIENTS

- 3 cups all-purpose flour
- ½ teaspoon baking soda
- ½ teaspoon salt
- ½ teaspoon baking powder
- 1 cup butter
- 2 large eggs eggs
- 1 cup white sugar
- 1 teaspoon rum flavored extract
- ½ teaspoon almond extract
- ⅛ teaspoon ground nutmeg

DIRECTIONS

Step 1

Mix together flour, baking soda, salt, baking powder, and butter until the mixture resembles cornmeal.

Step 2

Combine eggs, sugar, rum extract, almond extract, and nutmeg until well mixed. Pour the egg mixture into the flour mixture. Stir until well blended. Divide the dough into two equal halves. Refrigerate the dough for 2 hours.

Step 3

Preheat the oven to 350 degrees F (175 degrees C).

Step 4

Place dough on a lightly floured surface. Roll the dough out until it is 1/8 inch thick. Using a cookie cutter cut the dough into cookies (whatever shapes you please). Place the cookies on an ungreased baking sheet.

Step 5

Bake in the preheated oven until the edges are golden, 7 to 9 minutes. Allow the cookies to cool on the baking sheet for 1 minute before removing to a wire rack to cool completely.

TASTY EGGNOG COOKIES

INGREDIENTS

- 1 cup margarine
- 1 cup white sugar
- 1 egg
- 1 cup eggnog
- 3 ¼ cups all-purpose flour
- 1 teaspoon baking powder
- 1 teaspoon baking soda
- ½ teaspoon salt
- 1 ½ cups confectioners' sugar
- 3 tablespoons eggnog

DIRECTIONS

Step 1

Preheat oven to 350 degrees F (175 degrees C). Grease cookie sheets.

Step 2

In a medium bowl, cream together the margarine and white sugar until smooth. Stir in the egg and 1 cup eggnog. Combine the flour, baking powder, baking soda and salt; stir into the sugar mixture so it is well blended. Drop by rounded spoonfuls onto the prepared cookie sheet. Drop by rounded spoonfuls onto the prepared cookie sheets.

Step 3

Bake for 8 to 10 minutes in the preheated oven. Allow cookies to cool on baking sheet for 5 minutes before removing to a wire rack to cool completely.

Step 4

To prepare the icing, put the confectioners' sugar into a small bowl. Stir in the remaining eggnog one tablespoon at a time until the desired consistency is reached. Spread onto cooled cookies and let dry before serving.

WHITE CHOCOLATE-ORANGE-PISTACHIO THUMBPRINT COOKIES

INGREDIENTS

Cookies:

- 1 cup butter, softened
- ¼ cup white sugar
- 2 large egg yolks egg yolks
- ½ teaspoon vanilla extract
- 2 ½ cups all-purpose flour
- ¼ teaspoon salt
- 1 (3.4 ounce) package instant pistachio pudding mix

Filling:

- 2 cups white chocolate chips
- ¼ cup whole milk
- 1 tablespoon grated orange zest
- 2 ounces roasted, salted pistachios, finely chopped

DIRECTIONS

Step 1

Combine butter, sugar, egg yolks, and vanilla extract in large bowl. Beat using an electric mixer until well mixed. Add flour, salt, and pudding mix; beat well. Chill dough in the refrigerator for 30 minutes.

Step 2

Preheat the oven to 325 degrees F (165 degrees C). Line a baking sheet with parchment paper.

Step 3

Shape dough into 1-inch balls and place on the prepared baking sheets. Make an indentation in the center of each cookie with your thumb.

Step 4

Bake in the preheated oven until lightly golden around the edges, 10 to 12 minutes. Remove from baking sheet and allow to cool on a wire rack, about 30 minutes.

Step 5

Combine white chocolate chips, milk, and orange zest in a microwave-safe bowl. Heat in the microwave for 1 1/2 minutes, stirring every 30 seconds, until chocolate is melted and smooth.

Step 6

Pour white chocolate mixture into a piping bag and pipe into the thumbprint of the cooled cookies. Sprinkle with chopped pistachios.

FRUIT AND SPICE ROUNDS

Servings: 30 **Yield:** 5 dozen

INGREDIENTS

- 2 cups all-purpose flour
- 1 teaspoon baking soda
- 1 teaspoon salt
- 1 teaspoon ground cinnamon
- ¾ teaspoon ground cloves
- ½ teaspoon ground nutmeg
- 1 cup raisins
- 1 cup dried figs
- 1 cup pitted dates
- ½ cup chopped walnuts
- 1 cup butter
- 1 ½ cups white sugar
- 3 large eggs eggs
- 1 ½ cups sifted confectioners' sugar
- 1 tablespoon butter, softened
- ½ teaspoon vanilla extract
- 5 teaspoons milk

DIRECTIONS

Step 1

In a food processor or with the fine blade of a food grinder, process or grind raisins, figs, dates and walnuts.

Step 2

In a large mixing bowl beat butter until softened. Add sugar and beat until fluffy. Add eggs and beat well.

Step 3

In a mixing bowl stir together flour, baking soda, salt, cinnamon, cloves, and nutmeg. Add flour mixture and beat until well mixed.

Step 4

Stir in ground fruit mixture. Divide dough in half; cover and chill several hours or overnight.

Step 5

Preheat oven to 375 degrees F. Grease cookie sheet.

Step 6

On a well floured surface roll dough 1/4 inch thick. Cut into rounds with a 2 1/2-inch cookie cutter. Place on cookie sheet and bake for 10-12 minute or until done. Cool on cookie sheet for 2-3 minutes, then remove and cool thoroughly on rack.

Step 7

Combine 1 1/2 cups sifted powdered sugar, 1 tablespoon softened butter or margarine, and 1/2 teaspoon vanilla and enough milk (4-5 tsp) to make icing of drizzling consistency.

COOKIE IN A JAR

INGREDIENTS

- ½ cup white chocolate chips
- ½ cup crispy rice cereal
- 1 ½ cups all-purpose flour
- ¾ teaspoon baking soda
- ¼ teaspoon baking powder
- ½ cup packed brown sugar
- ½ cup semisweet chocolate chips
- ½ cup rolled oats
- ½ cup white sugar

DIRECTIONS

Step 1

In a 1 quart jar, layer the ingredients in the order listed. Pack down firmly after each addition.

Step 2

Attach a tag with the following instructions: Cookie in a Jar 1. Preheat the oven to 350 degrees F (175 degrees C). 2. In a large bowl, cream 1/2 cup margarine until light and fluffy. Mix in 1 egg and 2 tablespoons water. Add the entire contents of the jar, and stir until well blended. Drop by rounded spoonfuls onto an ungreased cookie sheet. 3. Bake for 10 to 12 minutes in preheated oven. Remove from baking sheets to cool on wire racks.

VANILLE KIPFERL

INGREDIENTS

- 2 cups all-purpose flour

- ⅓ cup white sugar
- ¾ cup ground almonds
- 1 cup unsalted butter
- ¼ cup vanilla sugar
- ¼ cup confectioners' sugar

DIRECTIONS

Step 1

Preheat oven to 325 degrees F (170 degrees C). Line a baking sheet with parchment paper.

Step 2

Combine flour, 1/3 cup sugar, and ground almonds. Cut in butter with pastry blender, then quickly knead into a dough.

Step 3

Shape dough into logs and cut off 1/2-inch pieces. Shape each piece into a crescent and place on prepared baking sheet.

Step 4

Bake in preheated oven until edges are golden brown, 8 to 10 minutes. Cool 1 minute and carefully roll in vanilla sugar mixture.

CAKE MIX GINGERBREAD MEN

INGREDIENTS

- 1 package Duncan Hines Moist Deluxe Spice Cake Mix
- 1 cup all-purpose flour
- 2 large eggs eggs
- ⅓ cup vegetable oil
- ⅓ cup dark molasses
- 2 teaspoons ground ginger
- non-pareils
- 1 tub Duncan Hines Creamy Home-Style Vanilla Icing
- heavy weight storage or freezer bag

DIRECTIONS

Step 1

Preheat oven to 375 degrees F.

Step 2

Combine cake mix, flour, eggs, oil, molasses and ginger in large bowl (mixture will be soft). Refrigerate 2 hours.

Step 3

Place dough on lightly floured surface, cover with waxed paper. Roll dough to 1/4-inch thickness. Cut with gingerbread man cookie cutter. Place 3 inches apart on ungreased cookie sheet. Decorate with non pareils.

Step 4

Bake 8 to 10 minutes or until edges start to brown. Remove immediately to cooling rack.

Step 5

Place icing in storage bag. Snip just the tip of one corner off to allow for a small hole. Pipe the face and ruffles onto cookies.

CHERRY MASH BARS

INGREDIENTS

- 2 tablespoons butter
- 1 cup white sugar
- ¼ teaspoon salt
- ⅓ cup half-and-half cream
- 1 cup miniature marshmallows
- 1 cup cherry baking chips
- 1 cup semisweet chocolate chips
- ½ cup peanut butter
- 1 cup roasted Spanish peanuts

DIRECTIONS

Step 1

Line an 8x8 or 9x9 inch square pan with waxed paper.

Step 2

In a medium saucepan, combine butter, sugar, salt and half and half. Heat until boiling, stirring occasionally. Boil for 5 minutes, stirring enough to keep from scorching. Remove from heat and stir in the marshmallows, and cherry chips. Press the mixture into the prepared pan.

Step 3

In the microwave or in a metal bowl over a pan of simmering water, melt chocolate chips, and peanut butter together stirring frequently until smooth. Spread over the mixture in the pan. Refrigerate for 2 hours before cutting into squares.

CRANBERRY CORNMEAL LINZER COOKIES

INGREDIENTS

Cookies:

- ¾ cup butter, softened
- ¾ cup white sugar
- 1 egg
- 1 ½ cups all-purpose flour
- ½ cup cornmeal
- 1 teaspoon baking powder

- ⅜ teaspoon salt
- 1 teaspoon vanilla extract

Filling:

- 1 ½ cups finely chopped cranberries
- ⅓ cup brown sugar
- ⅓ cup water
- 1 ½ tablespoons butter
- 1 ½ tablespoons lemon juice

DIRECTIONS

Step 1

Beat 3/4 cup butter and and white sugar together in a bowl with an electric mixer until creamy. Beat egg into butter mixture.

Step 2

Whisk flour, cornmeal, baking powder, and salt together in a bowl. Gradually add flour mixture to butter mixture; stir. Beat vanilla into butter mixture. Form dough into a ball, wrap tightly in plastic wrap, and refrigerate until firm, at least 1 hour.

Step 3

Preheat oven to 350 degrees F (175 degrees C). Lightly grease baking sheets.

Step 4

Roll dough out onto a lightly floured surface to 1/8-inch thick. Cut dough with a round or Linzer cookie cutter. Use a smaller cutter to cut the center from the tops. Place cookie bottoms and tops 1-inch apart on prepared baking sheets.

Step 5

Bake in the preheated oven until edges are lightly golden, 10 to 12 minutes. Transfer to wire racks to cool.

Step 6

Stir cranberries, brown sugar, and water together in a saucepan over medium-high heat; cook until cranberries are soft, about 10 minutes. Stir butter and lemon juice into cranberry mixture; remove from heat and cool.

Step 7

Spread a small amount of the cranberry mixture onto one side of the bottom half of a cookie. Place the top half of the cookie on top of the cranberry mixture. Repeat assembly process with remaining cookies and cranberry filling.

5% DV; sodium 61.5mg 3% DV.

Amaretti Italian Cookies

INGREDIENTS

- 5 cups finely chopped roasted almonds

- 2 cups white sugar
- 1 ½ teaspoons unsweetened cocoa powder
- 4 large eggs eggs
- 1 (1 ounce) bottle almond extract, or to taste
- ¼ cup white sugar
- 45 almonds whole almonds

DIRECTIONS

Step 1

Preheat oven to 350 degrees F (175 degrees C). Line 2 baking sheets with parchment paper.

Step 2

Mix chopped almonds, 2 cups white sugar, and cocoa powder together in a bowl; add eggs and almond extract and stir until batter is well mixed. Form teaspoonfuls of batter into small balls.

Step 3

Place 1/4 cup sugar in a bowl and roll balls in the sugar. Press a finger into the center of each ball, making an indentation. Place 1 almond in each indentation. Arrange cookies 2 inches apart on the baking sheets.

Step 4

Bake in the preheated oven until edges begin to crisp, about 15 minutes.

CHERRY-ALMOND ICEBOX COOKIES

INGREDIENTS

- 1 cup butter, softened
- 1 cup brown sugar
- 2 cups all-purpose flour
- ½ cup sliced blanched almonds
- ½ cup chopped red candied cherries
- 2 ounces white chocolate

DIRECTIONS

Step 1

Preheat oven to 350 degrees F (175 degrees C). Line bottom and sides of an 11x7-inch glass baking pan with parchment paper; leave paper hanging over pan edges so that cookies can be lifted out after baking.

Step 2

Beat butter and brown sugar together with an electric mixer until light and fluffy, about 2 minutes. Stir flour into butter mixture until crumbly; stir in almonds and cherries. Press mixture evenly into the bottom of prepared pan.

Step 3

Bake in the preheated oven until lightly golden at edges, about 20 minutes. Score with a sharp knife into bars while in the pan and still warm; allow cookies to cool about 30 minutes. Lift cookies from pan and slice to separate along scored marks.

Step 4

Melt white chocolate in a microwave-safe glass or ceramic bowl in 30-second intervals, stirring after each melting, for 1 to 3 minutes (depending on your microwave). Do not overheat or chocolate will scorch. Drizzle melted white chocolate over cookies or dip half of each cookie into melted white chocolate.

CHERRY BELL COOKIES

Servings: 30 **Yield:** 5 dozen

INGREDIENTS

- 3 cups all-purpose flour
- ½ teaspoon baking soda
- ½ teaspoon salt
- 1 teaspoon ground ginger
- ½ teaspoon instant coffee granules
- 1 cup butter
- 1 ¼ cups packed brown sugar
- ¼ cup dark corn syrup
- 1 egg, beaten
- 1 tablespoon cream
- ⅓ cup packed brown sugar
- 1 tablespoon butter
- 3 tablespoons cherry juice
- 1 ½ cups chopped walnuts
- 60 cherries maraschino cherries, halved

DIRECTIONS

Step 1

Sift together: 3 cups flour, 1/2 teaspoon baking soda, 1/2 teaspoon salt, 1 teaspoon ginger and 1/2 teaspoon instant coffee. Put aside.

Step 2

Cream 1 cup butter or margarine. Add 1 1/4 cups brown sugar. Cream well. Blend in dark corn syrup, egg, and cream. Add dry ingredients and mix well.

Step 3

Roll out dough, 1/3 at a time on floured board to 1/8 inch thickness. Cut cookies into 2 1/2 inch rounds. Place on ungreased cookie sheet.

Step 4

To Make Filling: Combine 1/3 firmly packed brown sugar, 1 tablespoon butter, 3 tablespoons cherry juice. Stir in 1 1/2 cups chopped nuts, chopped fine.

Step 5

Place 1/2 teaspoon filling in center of each round. Shape into a bell by folding sides of dough to meet over the filling using spatula to fold over sides. Make top of bell narrower than at the clapper end. Place

1/2 of a maraschino cherry (cut side down) at open end of each bell for clapper. Bake at 350 degrees F for 12-15 minutes.

Basic Gingersnap Cookies

INGREDIENTS

- 6 cups all-purpose flour
- 1 teaspoon baking soda
- ½ teaspoon baking powder
- 1 ½ teaspoons salt
- 4 teaspoons ground ginger
- 4 teaspoons ground cinnamon
- 1 ½ teaspoons ground cloves
- 1 teaspoon ground black pepper
- 1 cup unsalted butter, softened
- 1 cup packed brown sugar
- 2 large eggs eggs
- 1 cup unsulfured molasses

DIRECTIONS

Step 1

Sift together the flour, baking soda, baking powder, salt, ginger, cinnamon, cloves, and black pepper; set aside. In a large bowl, or stand mixer with the paddle attachment, cream together the butter and sugar until smooth. Beat in the eggs one at a time, then stir in the molasses. Gradually mix in the sifted ingredients. Divide the dough into thirds and wrap in plastic wrap. Refrigerate for at least one hour.

Step 2

Preheat oven to 350 degrees F (175 degrees C).

Step 3

On a lightly floured surface, roll the dough out to 1/8 inch in thickness. Cut into desired shapes with cookie cutters. Place cookies 1 1/2 inches apart onto cookie sheets.

Step 4

Bake for 8 to 10 minutes in the preheated oven, until cookies are crisp but not dark. Remove to wire racks to cool completely. Decorate as desired.

RUSSIAN TEA CAKES

INGREDIENTS

- 1 cup unsalted butter, room temperature
- 1 ⅓ cups confectioners' sugar, divided
- 1 cup finely chopped toasted walnuts
- ⅛ teaspoon salt
- 1 teaspoon vanilla extract
- 2 cups all-purpose flour

- 2 tablespoons all-purpose flour
- 1 cup confectioners' sugar for dusting, or more as needed

DIRECTIONS

Step 1

Preheat oven to 350 degrees F (175 degrees C). Arrange rack in center position of oven.

Step 2

Place butter, 1/3 cup packed powdered sugar, walnuts, salt, and vanilla in a bowl. Top with the flour. Mix with your clean hands until the dough starts to clump up. Keep mixing by hand until all the flour and clumps of butter are evenly mixed into the dough and it can be easily formed into balls.

Step 3

Scoop out dough and roll by hand into uniformly round balls, just slightly larger than 1 inch. Place on a rimmed baking sheet lined with a silicone baking mat about 2 inches apart.

Step 4

Bake in preheated oven until lightly golden, 15 to 25 minutes depending on the size of the cookies.

Step 5

Let cool exactly 5 minutes then roll in remaining 1 cup confectioners' sugar. Let cookies cool completely and toss them again in the confectioners' sugar.

HEDGEHOG COOKIES

INGREDIENTS

- 4 cups all-purpose flour
- ¾ teaspoon baking powder
- ½ teaspoon baking soda
- ½ teaspoon salt
- 1 ¼ cups white sugar
- 1 cup butter-flavored shortening
- ¼ cup corn syrup
- 2 large eggs eggs
- 1 tablespoon vanilla extract
- 1 cup pecans
- 1 cup chocolate chips

DIRECTIONS

Step 1

Mix flour, baking powder, baking soda, and salt in a bowl. Whisk sugar, shortening, corn syrup, eggs, and vanilla extract in a separate bowl. Stir sugar mixture into flour mixture until just combined. Refrigerate dough until chilled, 30 minutes to 1 hour.

Step 2

Preheat oven to 350 degrees F (175 degrees C).

Step 3

Scoop cookie dough using a cookie scoop or 1 tablespoon so all the cookies are uniform; shape dough into teardrop-shaped cookies. Flatten the pointed side of each cookie to form the 'face'. Arrange cookies on baking sheets.

Step 4

Bake in the preheated oven until golden, 10 to 12 minutes. Cool on the baking sheets for 10 minutes before removing to cool completely on a wire rack.

Step 5

Pulse pecans in a food processor until finely chopped; transfer to a bowl.

Step 6

Melt chocolate chips in the top of a double boiler over simmering water, stirring frequently and scraping down the sides with a rubber spatula to avoid scorching.

Step 7

Dip the top of each cookie in the melted chocolate, spreading to fully coat the 'body' of each hedgehog. Press cookies, chocolate-side down, into the ground pecans forming the 'fur'. Arrange cookies on a sheet of waxed paper to set, about 30 minutes.

Step 8

Transfer the remaining melted chocolate to a piping bag or plastic bag with a corner snipped. Pipe chocolate onto the pointed end of each cookie for eyes and a nose.

ROYAL ICING

INGREDIENTS

- 3 tablespoons meringue powder
- 4 cups sifted confectioners' sugar
- 6 tablespoons water

DIRECTIONS

Step 1

Beat all ingredients at low speed for 7 to 10 minutes, or until icing forms peaks. Tip: Keep icing covered with a wet kitchen towel at all times. Icing can dry out quickly.

RUSSIAN TEA CAKES

INGREDIENTS

- 1 cup butter
- 1 teaspoon vanilla extract
- 6 tablespoons confectioners' sugar
- 2 cups all-purpose flour
- 1 cup chopped walnuts
- $\frac{1}{3}$ cup confectioners' sugar for decoration

DIRECTIONS

Step 1

Preheat oven to 350 degrees F (175 degrees C).

Step 2

In a medium bowl, cream butter and vanilla until smooth. Combine the 6 tablespoons confectioners' sugar and flour; stir into the butter mixture until just blended. Mix in the chopped walnuts. Roll dough into 1 inch balls, and place them 2 inches apart on an ungreased cookie sheet.

Step 3

Bake for 12 minutes in the preheated oven. When cool, roll in remaining confectioners' sugar. I also like to roll mine in the sugar a second time.

CHOCOLATE PEPPERMINT BISCOTTI

INGREDIENTS

- 2 cups white sugar
- 1 cup butter, softened
- 1 cup unsweetened cocoa powder
- 4 large eggs eggs
- ⅓ cup chocolate liqueur (such as Godiva)
- 2 teaspoons peppermint extract
- 4 ½ cups all-purpose flour
- 4 teaspoons baking powder
- ¾ teaspoon salt
- 1 ⅔ cups mint chocolate chips (such as Hershey's)
- 2 (14 ounce) packages white candy melts (confectioners' coating)
- 6 eaches large peppermint candy canes, crushed

DIRECTIONS

Step 1

Preheat oven to 350 degrees F (175 degrees C). Line two baking sheets with parchment paper.

Step 2

Beat white sugar, butter, and cocoa powder together with an electric mixer in a large bowl until creamy and smooth. Add eggs, one at a time, beating well after each addition. Mix chocolate liqueur and peppermint extract into the sugar-egg mixture.

Step 3

Combine flour, baking powder, and salt in a separate bowl. Slowly mix flour mixture into sugar-egg mixture until fully incorporated; fold mint chocolate chips into the dough.

Step 4

Divide dough into 4 equal parts and shape into logs. Arrange the logs on the prepared baking sheets.

Step 5

Dip a spatula in water and use it to smooth surface of the logs.

Step 6

Bake biscotti logs in the preheated oven until firm to the touch, 30 to 35 minutes. Cool biscotti logs completely on wire racks.

Step 7

Reduce oven temperature to 300 degrees F (150 degrees C).

Step 8

Cut biscotti logs into 3/4-inch slices and arrange on baking sheets.

Step 9

Bake in the oven until biscotti are dry, about 10 minutes per side. Cool completely on wire racks.

Step 10

Place candy melts in a wide microwave-safe bowl; heat in microwave until melted, about 2 1/2 minutes, stirring every 30 seconds.

Step 11

Dip cooled biscotti in the melted white candy; sprinkle with crushed candy canes.

CHOCOLATE RUM BALLS

INGREDIENTS

- 3 ¼ cups crushed vanilla wafers
- ¾ cup confectioners' sugar
- ¼ cup unsweetened cocoa powder
- 1 ½ cups chopped walnuts
- 3 tablespoons light corn syrup
- ½ cup rum

DIRECTIONS

Step 1

In a large bowl, stir together the crushed vanilla wafers, 3/4 cup confectioners' sugar, cocoa, and nuts. Blend in corn syrup and rum.

Step 2

Shape into 1 inch balls, and roll in additional confectioners' sugar. Store in an airtight container for several days to develop the flavor. Roll again in confectioners' sugar before serving.

CITRUS SHORTBREAD COOKIES

INGREDIENTS

- 2 cups all-purpose flour
- ¼ teaspoon baking powder
- ⅛ teaspoon salt
- 1 cup butter, softened
- ¾ cup confectioners' sugar

- 2 teaspoons vanilla extract
- ½ teaspoon almond extract
- 1 tablespoon grated orange zest, or more to taste
- 2 cups sweetened dried cranberries, chopped

DIRECTIONS

Step 1

Combine flour, baking powder, and salt in a bowl; set aside. Beat the butter and confectioners' sugar with an electric mixer in a large bowl until smooth. Stir in the vanilla and almond extracts and orange zest. Mix in the flour mixture until just incorporated. Fold in the cranberries; mixing just enough to evenly combine.

Step 2

Divide the dough into 2 equal portions, then roll into logs about 7 inches long. Wrap each log in wax paper or plastic wrap, and chill in the refrigerator for at least 4 hours.

Step 3

Preheat an oven to 350 degrees F (175 degrees C).

Step 4

Remove wax paper, and cut the cookie dough into 1/2-inch slices. Arrange the slices on a baking sheet about 1 inch apart.

Step 5

Bake in the preheated oven until firm but not browned, about 10 minutes.

Crescent Butter Biscuits

INGREDIENTS

- 2 ½ cups all-purpose flour
- 1 ¾ cups almond flour
- ¾ cup white sugar
- 1 cup butter
- 3 large egg yolks egg yolks
- 1 tablespoon vanilla sugar, or as needed

DIRECTIONS

Step 1

Combine all-purpose flour, almond flour, and sugar in a bowl; rub in butter using your fingers until coarse crumbs form. Add egg yolks and work into a smooth dough. Wrap dough in plastic wrap and chill in the refrigerator for 1 hour.

Step 2

Preheat oven to 350 degrees F (175 degrees C). Line a baking sheet with parchment paper.

Step 3

Turn dough onto a floured work surface; roll into long, thin pieces. Cut into 2-inch pieces and shape each piece into a crescent-shape. Place crescents on the prepared baking sheet.

Step 4

Bake in preheated oven until lightly golden, 10 to 15 minutes. Immediately roll the crescents in vanilla sugar while hot. Set aside to cool.

BEST CHOCOLATE CHIP COOKIES

INGREDIENTS

- 1 cup butter, softened
- 1 cup white sugar
- 1 cup packed brown sugar
- 2 large eggs eggs
- 2 teaspoons vanilla extract
- 1 teaspoon baking soda
- 2 teaspoons hot water
- ½ teaspoon salt
- 3 cups all-purpose flour
- 2 cups semisweet chocolate chips
- 1 cup chopped walnuts

DIRECTIONS

Step 1

Preheat oven to 350 degrees F (175 degrees C).

Step 2

Cream together the butter, white sugar, and brown sugar until smooth. Beat in the eggs one at a time, then stir in the vanilla. Dissolve baking soda in hot water. Add to batter along with salt. Stir in flour, chocolate chips, and nuts. Drop by large spoonfuls onto ungreased pans.

Step 3

Bake for about 10 minutes in the preheated oven, or until edges are nicely browned.

EASY SUGAR COOKIES

INGREDIENTS

- 2 ¾ cups all-purpose flour
- 1 teaspoon baking soda
- ½ teaspoon baking powder
- 1 cup butter, softened
- 1 ½ cups white sugar
- 1 egg
- 1 teaspoon vanilla extract

DIRECTIONS

Step 1

Preheat oven to 375 degrees F (190 degrees C). In a small bowl, stir together flour, baking soda, and baking powder. Set aside.

Step 2

In a large bowl, cream together the butter and sugar until smooth. Beat in egg and vanilla. Gradually blend in the dry ingredients. Roll rounded teaspoonfuls of dough into balls, and place onto ungreased cookie sheets.

Step 3

Bake 8 to 10 minutes in the preheated oven, or until golden. Let stand on cookie sheet two minutes before removing to cool on wire racks.

BEST BIG, FAT, CHEWY CHOCOLATE CHIP COOKIE

INGREDIENTS

- 2 cups all-purpose flour
- ½ teaspoon baking soda
- ½ teaspoon salt
- ¾ cup unsalted butter, melted
- 1 cup packed brown sugar
- ½ cup white sugar
- 1 tablespoon vanilla extract
- 1 egg
- 1 egg yolk
- 2 cups semisweet chocolate chips

DIRECTIONS

Step 1

Preheat the oven to 325 degrees F (165 degrees C). Grease cookie sheets or line with parchment paper.

Step 2

Sift together the flour, baking soda and salt; set aside.

Step 3

In a medium bowl, cream together the melted butter, brown sugar and white sugar until well blended. Beat in the vanilla, egg, and egg yolk until light and creamy. Mix in the sifted ingredients until just blended. Stir in the chocolate chips by hand using a wooden spoon. Drop cookie dough 1/4 cup at a time onto the prepared cookie sheets. Cookies should be about 3 inches apart.

Step 4

Bake for 15 to 17 minutes in the preheated oven, or until the edges are lightly toasted. Cool on baking sheets for a few minutes before transferring to wire racks to cool completely.

ICED PUMPKIN COOKIES

INGREDIENTS

- 2 ½ cups all-purpose flour
- 1 teaspoon baking powder
- 1 teaspoon baking soda
- 2 teaspoons ground cinnamon
- ½ teaspoon ground nutmeg
- ½ teaspoon ground cloves
- ½ teaspoon salt
- ½ cup butter, softened
- 1 ½ cups white sugar
- 1 cup canned pumpkin puree
- 1 egg
- 1 teaspoon vanilla extract
- 2 cups confectioners' sugar
- 3 tablespoons milk
- 1 tablespoon melted butter
- 1 teaspoon vanilla extract

DIRECTIONS

Step 1

Preheat oven to 350 degrees F (175 degrees C). Combine flour, baking powder, baking soda, cinnamon, nutmeg, ground cloves, and salt; set aside.

Step 2

In a medium bowl, cream together the 1/2 cup of butter and white sugar. Add pumpkin, egg, and 1 teaspoon vanilla to butter mixture, and beat until creamy. Mix in dry ingredients. Drop on cookie sheet by tablespoonfuls; flatten slightly.

Step 3

Bake for 15 to 20 minutes in the preheated oven. Cool cookies, then drizzle glaze with fork.

Step 4

To Make Glaze: Combine confectioners' sugar, milk, 1 tablespoon melted butter, and 1 teaspoon vanilla. Add milk as needed, to achieve drizzling consistency.

THE BEST ROLLED SUGAR COOKIES

INGREDIENTS

- 1 ½ cups butter, softened
- 2 cups white sugar
- 4 large eggs eggs
- 1 teaspoon vanilla extract
- 5 cups all-purpose flour
- 2 teaspoons baking powder
- 1 teaspoon salt

DIRECTIONS

Step 1

In a large bowl, cream together butter and sugar until smooth. Beat in eggs and vanilla. Stir in the flour, baking powder, and salt. Cover, and chill dough for at least one hour (or overnight).

Step 2

Preheat oven to 400 degrees F (200 degrees C). Roll out dough on floured surface 1/4 to 1/2 inch thick. Cut into shapes with any cookie cutter. Place cookies 1 inch apart on ungreased cookie sheets.

Step 3

Bake 6 to 8 minutes in preheated oven. Cool completely.

BIG SOFT GINGER COOKIES

INGREDIENTS

- 2 ¼ cups all-purpose flour
- 2 teaspoons ground ginger
- 1 teaspoon baking soda
- ¾ teaspoon ground cinnamon
- ½ teaspoon ground cloves
- ¼ teaspoon salt
- ¾ cup margarine, softened
- 1 cup white sugar
- 1 egg
- 1 tablespoon water
- ¼ cup molasses
- 2 tablespoons white sugar

DIRECTIONS

Step 1

Preheat oven to 350 degrees F (175 degrees C). Sift together the flour, ginger, baking soda, cinnamon, cloves, and salt. Set aside.

Step 2

In a large bowl, cream together the margarine and 1 cup sugar until light and fluffy. Beat in the egg, then stir in the water and molasses. Gradually stir the sifted ingredients into the molasses mixture. Shape dough into walnut sized balls, and roll them in the remaining 2 tablespoons of sugar. Place the cookies 2 inches apart onto an ungreased cookie sheet, and flatten slightly.

Step 3

Bake for 8 to 10 minutes in the preheated oven. Allow cookies to cool on baking sheet for 5 minutes before removing to a wire rack to cool completely. Store in an airtight container.

MACARON (FRENCH MACAROON)

INGREDIENTS

- 3 large egg whites egg whites
- ¼ cup white sugar

- 1 ⅔ cups confectioners' sugar
- 1 cup finely ground almonds

DIRECTIONS

Step 1

Line a baking sheet with a silicone baking mat.

Step 2

Beat egg whites in the bowl of a stand mixer fitted with a whisk attachment until whites are foamy; beat in white sugar and continue beating until egg whites are glossy, fluffy, and hold soft peaks. Sift confectioners' sugar and ground almonds in a separate bowl and quickly fold the almond mixture into the egg whites, about 30 strokes.

Step 3

Spoon a small amount of batter into a plastic bag with a small corner cut off and pipe a test disk of batter, about 1 1/2 inches in diameter, onto prepared baking sheet. If the disk of batter holds a peak instead of flattening immediately, gently fold the batter a few more times and retest.

Step 4

When batter is mixed enough to flatten immediately into an even disk, spoon into a pastry bag fitted with a plain round tip. Pipe the batter onto the baking sheet in rounds, leaving space between the disks. Let the piped cookies stand out at room temperature until they form a hard skin on top, about 1 hour.

Step 5

Preheat oven to 285 degrees F (140 degrees C).

Step 6

Bake cookies until set but not browned, about 10 minutes; let cookies cool completely before filling.

PEANUT BUTTER BARS

INGREDIENTS

- 1 cup butter or margarine, melted
- 2 cups graham cracker crumbs
- 2 cups confectioners' sugar
- 1 cup peanut butter
- 1 ½ cups semisweet chocolate chips
- 4 tablespoons peanut butter

DIRECTIONS

Step 1

In a medium bowl, mix together the butter or margarine, graham cracker crumbs, confectioners' sugar, and 1 cup peanut butter until well blended. Press evenly into the bottom of an ungreased 9x13 inch pan.

Step 2

In a metal bowl over simmering water, or in the microwave, melt the chocolate chips with the 4 tablespoons peanut butter, stirring occasionally until smooth. Spread over the prepared crust. Refrigerate for at least one hour before cutting into squares.

BISCOTTI

INGREDIENTS

- ½ cup vegetable oil
- 1 cup white sugar
- 3 ¼ cups all-purpose flour
- 3 large eggs eggs
- 1 tablespoon baking powder
- 1 tablespoon anise extract, or 3 drops anise oil

DIRECTIONS

Step 1

Preheat the oven to 375 degrees F (190 degrees C). Grease cookie sheets or line with parchment paper.

Step 2

In a medium bowl, beat together the oil, eggs, sugar and anise flavoring until well blended. Combine the flour and baking powder, stir into the egg mixture to form a heavy dough. Divide dough into two pieces. Form each piece into a roll as long as your cookie sheet. Place roll onto the prepared cookie sheet, and press down to 1/2 inch thickness.

Step 3

Bake for 25 to 30 minutes in the preheated oven, until golden brown. Remove from the baking sheet to cool on a wire rack. When The cookies are cool enough to handle, slice each one crosswise into 1/2 inch slices. Place the slices cut side up back onto the baking sheet. Bake for an additional 6 to 10 minutes on each side. Slices should be lightly toasted.

AWARD WINNING SOFT CHOCOLATE CHIP COOKIES

INGREDIENTS

- 4 ½ cups all-purpose flour
- 2 teaspoons baking soda
- 2 cups butter, softened
- 1 ½ cups packed brown sugar
- ½ cup white sugar
- 2 (3.4 ounce) packages instant vanilla pudding mix
- 4 large eggs eggs
- 2 teaspoons vanilla extract
- 4 cups semisweet chocolate chips
- 2 cups chopped walnuts

DIRECTIONS

Step 1

Preheat oven to 350 degrees F (175 degrees C). Sift together the flour and baking soda, set aside.

Step 2

In a large bowl, cream together the butter, brown sugar, and white sugar. Beat in the instant pudding mix until blended. Stir in the eggs and vanilla. Blend in the flour mixture. Finally, stir in the chocolate chips and nuts. Drop cookies by rounded spoonfuls onto ungreased cookie sheets.

Step 3

Bake for 10 to 12 minutes in the preheated oven. Edges should be golden brown.

BROOKE'S BEST BOMBSHELL BROWNIES

INGREDIENTS

- 1 cup butter, melted
- 3 cups white sugar
- 1 tablespoon vanilla extract
- 4 large eggs eggs
- 1 ½ cups all-purpose flour
- 1 cup unsweetened cocoa powder
- 1 teaspoon salt
- 1 cup semisweet chocolate chips

DIRECTIONS

Step 1

Preheat oven to 350 degrees F (175 degrees C). Lightly grease a 9x13 baking dish.

Step 2

Combine the melted butter, sugar, and vanilla in a large bowl. Beat in the eggs, one at a time, mixing well after each, until thoroughly blended.

Step 3

Sift the flour, cocoa powder, and salt in a bowl. Gradually stir flour mixture into the egg mixture until blended. Stir in the chocolate morsels. Spread the batter evenly into the prepared baking dish.

Step 4

Bake in preheated oven until an inserted toothpick comes out clean, 35 to 40 minutes. Remove, and cool pan on wire rack before cutting.

COCONUT MACAROONS

INGREDIENTS

- ⅔ cup all-purpose flour
- 5 ½ cups flaked coconut
- ¼ teaspoon salt
- 1 (14 ounce) can sweetened condensed milk

- 2 teaspoons vanilla extract

DIRECTIONS

Step 1

Preheat oven to 350 degrees F (175 degrees C). Line cookie sheets with parchment paper or aluminum foil.

Step 2

In a large bowl, stir together the flour, coconut and salt. Stir in the sweetened condensed milk and vanilla using your hands until well blended. Use an ice cream scoop to drop dough onto the prepared cookie sheets. Cookies should be about golf ball size.

Step 3

Bake for 12 to 15 minutes in the preheated oven, until coconut is toasted.

NANAIMO BARS

INGREDIENTS

- ½ cup butter, softened
- ¼ cup white sugar
- 5 tablespoons unsweetened cocoa powder
- 1 egg, beaten
- 1 ¾ cups graham cracker crumbs
- 1 cup flaked coconut
- ½ cup finely chopped almonds
- ½ cup butter, softened
- 3 tablespoons heavy cream
- 2 tablespoons custard powder
- 2 cups confectioners' sugar
- 4 (1 ounce) squares semisweet baking chocolate
- 2 teaspoons butter

DIRECTIONS

Step 1

In the top of a double boiler, combine 1/2 cup butter, white sugar and cocoa powder. Stir occasionally until melted and smooth. Beat in the egg, stirring until thick, 2 to 3 minutes. Remove from heat and mix in the graham cracker crumbs, coconut and almonds (if you like). Press into the bottom of an ungreased 8x8 inch pan.

Step 2

For the middle layer, cream together 1/2 cup butter, heavy cream and custard powder until light and fluffy. Mix in the confectioners' sugar until smooth. Spread over the bottom layer in the pan. Chill to set.

Step 3

While the second layer is chilling, melt the semisweet chocolate and 2 teaspoons butter together in the microwave or over low heat. Spread over the chilled bars. Let the chocolate set before cutting into squares.

ALMOND MERINGUE COOKIES

INGREDIENTS

- 11 ounces ground almonds
- 3 large egg whites egg whites
- 1 cup confectioners' sugar
- 1 teaspoon grated lemon zest
- ¾ teaspoon ground cinnamon

DIRECTIONS

Step 1

Preheat the oven to 325 degrees F (165 degrees C). Grease and lightly flour cookie sheets.

Step 2

In a large bowl, whip egg whites until soft peaks form. Gradually sprinkle in the sugar and keep whipping until the egg whites can hold a stiff peak, this will take about 5 minutes. Set aside about 1/2 cup of the egg whites. Add the lemon zest and cinnamon to the rest of the meringue, and fold in the almonds until everything is evenly blended.

Step 3

Drop mounds by spoonfuls onto the prepared baking sheets. Top each cookie with a smaller dollop of the reserved meringue.

Step 4

Bake for 15 minutes in the preheated oven, until golden brown. Remove cookies from the baking sheets to cool on wire racks.

BON BON CHRISTMAS COOKIES

Servings: 24 **Yield:** 2 dozen

INGREDIENTS

- ½ (8 ounce) package cream cheese
- ½ cup butter flavored shortening
- 2 cups sifted all-purpose flour
- 1 ½ cups sifted confectioners' sugar
- 2 (10 ounce) jars maraschino cherries, drained

DIRECTIONS

Step 1

In a medium bowl, stir together the shortening and cream cheese until well blended. Stir in the flour, you may need to use your hands to help it form a dough. If the mixture seems too dry, add a couple of teaspoons of water. Cover and chill several hours or overnight.

Step 2

Preheat the oven to 375 degrees F (190 degrees C). Lightly grease cookie sheets.

Step 3

Before rolling out the dough, dust the rolling surface heavily with confectioners' sugar. Roll the dough out to 1/8 inch thickness. Cut into 1x4 inch strips. Place a cherry on the end of each strip. Roll up each strip starting with the cherry. Place on prepared cookie sheets and dust with a little of the confectioners' sugar.

Step 4

Bake for 7 to 10 minutes in the preheated oven. Cookies should brown slightly. Dust again with the confectioners' sugar. Allow cookies to cool before serving, the cherries are very hot!

HOLLY CHRISTMAS COOKIES

INGREDIENTS

- 1 (16 ounce) package large marshmallows
- ½ cup butter, softened
- 1 ½ teaspoons vanilla extract
- 1 ½ teaspoons green food coloring
- 4 ½ cups cornflakes cereal
- 1 (2.25 ounce) package cinnamon red hot candies

DIRECTIONS

Step 1

In a saucepan over low heat, melt together the marshmallows, butter, vanilla, and food coloring. Mix in the cornflakes cereal.

Step 2

Drop by spoonfuls on wax paper, and decorate with red hots. Set aside, and allow to cool.

RUM BALLS

Servings: 36 **Yield:** 36 balls

INGREDIENTS

- 3 cups vanilla wafer crumbs
- ½ cup ground pecans
- 3 tablespoons cocoa
- 1 cup confectioners' sugar
- 3 tablespoons light corn syrup
- ⅓ cup water
- 2 teaspoons rum flavored extract
- ¼ cup confectioners' sugar

DIRECTIONS

Step 1

In a medium bowl, mix vanilla wafer crumbs, ground pecans, cocoa, 1 cup confectioners' sugar, corn syrup, water, and rum flavoring together.

Step 2

Roll mixture into 1 inch balls, and then roll in remaining confectioners' sugar. Store, covered, about a week before serving.

CHEWY NOELS

INGREDIENTS

- 2 tablespoons butter
- 1 cup packed brown sugar
- 5 tablespoons all-purpose flour
- ⅛ teaspoon baking soda
- 2 large eggs eggs, beaten
- 1 teaspoon vanilla extract
- 1 cup chopped walnuts
- ¼ cup confectioners' sugar for dusting

DIRECTIONS

Step 1

Preheat oven to 350 degrees F (175 degrees C). Melt the butter in a 7x11 inch baking dish, and tilt the pan to coat all of the sides; set aside.

Step 2

In a medium bowl, stir together the brown sugar, flour, and baking soda. Mix in the eggs and vanilla until smooth, then stir in the walnuts. Pour over the melted butter.

Step 3

Bake in the preheated oven for 20 minutes, or until the edges begin to brown. Cool, then cut into squares, and dust with confectioners sugar.

COCONUT RUM BALLS

INGREDIENTS

- 1 (12 ounce) package vanilla wafers, crushed
- 1 ⅓ cups flaked coconut
- 1 cup finely chopped walnuts
- 1 (14 ounce) can sweetened condensed milk
- ¼ cup rum
- ⅛ cup confectioners' sugar

DIRECTIONS

Step 1

In a large bowl, combine crumbs, coconut, & nuts. Add sweetened condensed milk & rum; mix well. Chill 4 hours.

Step 2

Shape into 1- inch balls. Roll in sugar. Store in covered container in refrigerator 24 hours before serving.

RASPBERRY THUMBPRINTS WITH WHITE CHOCOLATE GLAZE

INGREDIENTS

- ½ cup butter, softened
- ½ cup sour cream
- 1 cup white sugar
- 2 tablespoons milk
- 2 large eggs eggs
- 2 ⅔ cups all-purpose flour
- 2 cups rolled oats
- 1 teaspoon baking soda
- 5 ounces white chocolate, chopped
- ⅔ cup raspberry preserves
- 1 tablespoon butter
- ½ (1 ounce) square white chocolate
- 1 cup confectioners' sugar
- 2 tablespoons milk

DIRECTIONS

Step 1

Preheat oven to 350 degrees F (175 degrees C).

Step 2

In a large bowl, cream together the 1/2 cup butter and sugar until smooth. Blend in the sour cream, 2 tablespoons of milk and eggs. Combine the flour, oats and baking soda, gradually stir into the creamed mixture. Finally, stir in the chopped white chocolate. Drop by rounded spoonfuls onto the prepared cookie sheet. Using a finger or your thumb, press a dent into the center of each cookie. Fill the dent with a 1/2 teaspoon of raspberry preserves.

Step 3

Bake for 8 to 10 minutes in the preheated oven. Allow cookies to cool on baking sheet for 5 minutes before removing to a wire rack to cool completely.

Step 4

To make the glaze: Combine 1 tablespoon butter and 1/2 ounce white chocolate in a microwave safe bowl. cook on high, stirring every 15 seconds until smooth. Gradually beat in the confectioners' sugar and milk until icing is of a drizzling consistency. Drizzle over cooled cookies.

GINGERBREAD PEOPLE FROM JELL-O

INGREDIENTS

- ¾ cup butter, softened
- ¾ cup packed brown sugar

- 1 (3.4 ounce) package JELL-O Butterscotch Instant Pudding
- 1 egg
- 2 cups flour
- 1 teaspoon baking soda
- 1 tablespoon ground ginger
- 1 ½ teaspoons ground cinnamon

DIRECTIONS

Step 1

Beat butter, sugar, dry pudding mix and egg in large bowl with mixer until well blended. Mix remaining ingredients. Gradually add to butter mixture, beating well after each addition. Refrigerate 1 hour or until firm.

Step 2

Heat oven to 350 degrees F. Roll out dough on lightly floured surface to 1/4-inch thickness; cut into gingerbread shapes with 4-inch cookie cutter, re-rolling trimmings. Place, 2 inches apart, on baking sheets sprayed with cooking spray. Use straw to make hole near top of each cutout.

Step 3

Bake 10 to 12 min. or until edges are lightly browned. Cool on baking sheets 3 min. Remove to wire racks; cool completely. Decorate as desired. Insert ribbon through holes to hang cookies on tree.

ANISE DROPS

INGREDIENTS

- 3 large eggs eggs, beaten
- 1 cup white sugar
- 2 cups all-purpose flour
- ½ teaspoon baking powder
- ½ teaspoon cream of tartar
- 1 tablespoon anise seed

DIRECTIONS

Step 1

Preheat oven to 350 degrees F (175 degrees C).

Step 2

Combine the sugar and the beaten eggs and continue to beat for 15 minutes. Stir in the flour, baking powder, cream of tartar and the anise seeds.

Step 3

Drop by teaspoonfuls onto a greased cookie sheet and bake at 350 degrees F (175 degrees C) for 15 minutes.

PFEFFERNUESSE

INGREDIENTS

- 4 cups all-purpose flour
- ½ cup white sugar
- 1 ¼ teaspoons baking soda
- 1 ½ teaspoons ground cinnamon
- 1 teaspoon ground cloves
- 1 teaspoon ground nutmeg
- ½ teaspoon ground allspice
- 1 dash ground black pepper
- ¾ cup molasses
- ½ cup butter
- 2 large eggs eggs, beaten
- 1 ½ cups confectioners' sugar

DIRECTIONS

Step 1

In a large bowl, stir together the flour, sugar, baking soda, cinnamon, cloves, nutmeg and allspice. In a medium saucepan over medium heat, combine molasses and butter. Heat, stirring occasionally, until the butter is melted. Remove from heat and allow to cool to room temperature. When the mixture has cooled, beat in the eggs. Blend the molasses mixture into the dry ingredients until evenly mixed. Cover and refrigerate for at least 3 to 4 hours.

Step 2

Preheat oven to 350 degrees F (175 degrees C). Grease cookie sheets. Roll dough into 1 inch balls and place them 2 inches apart onto the cookie sheets.

Step 3

Bake for 12 to 14 minutes in the preheated oven, or until firm. While cookies are still warm, toss them in a bag with confectioners' sugar and toss to coat. When cool, toss with sugar again.

PEANUT BUTTER CUP COOKIES

INGREDIENTS

- 1 ¾ cups all-purpose flour
- ½ teaspoon salt
- 1 teaspoon baking soda
- ½ cup butter, softened
- ½ cup white sugar
- ½ cup peanut butter
- ½ cup packed brown sugar
- 1 egg, beaten
- 1 teaspoon vanilla extract
- 2 tablespoons milk
- 40 eaches miniature chocolate covered peanut butter cups, unwrapped

DIRECTIONS

Step 1

Preheat oven to 375 degrees F (190 degrees C). Sift together the flour, salt and baking soda; set aside.

Step 2

Cream together the butter, sugar, peanut butter and brown sugar until fluffy. Beat in the egg, vanilla and milk. Add the flour mixture; mix well. Shape into 40 balls and place each into an ungreased mini muffin pan.

Step 3

Bake at 375 degrees for about 8 minutes. Remove from oven and immediately press a mini peanut butter cup into each ball. Cool and carefully remove from pan.

SCOTCHAROOS

INGREDIENTS

- 1 cup light corn syrup
- 1 cup white sugar
- 1 ½ cups peanut butter
- 6 cups crisp rice cereal
- ½ cup semisweet chocolate chips
- ½ cup butterscotch chips

DIRECTIONS

Step 1

Generously butter a 9x13 inch baking pan. Set aside.

Step 2

In a large pot, mix together corn syrup, sugar, and peanut butter. Cook over medium heat, stirring until peanut butter melts. Bring mixture to a boil. Remove from heat, and stir in crisp rice cereal.

Step 3

Transfer mixture into a well buttered 9x13 inch pan. With your hands well buttered, pat it down into pan.

Step 4

In a medium saucepan, over medium low heat, melt chocolate chips and butterscotch chips until smooth. Spread over top of bars and let bars cool. Cut into squares.

MOLASSES COOKIES

INGREDIENTS

- ¾ cup margarine, melted
- 1 cup white sugar
- 1 egg
- ¼ cup molasses
- 2 cups all-purpose flour
- 2 teaspoons baking soda
- ½ teaspoon salt

- 1 teaspoon ground cinnamon
- ½ teaspoon ground cloves
- ½ teaspoon ground ginger
- ½ cup white sugar

DIRECTIONS

Step 1

In a medium bowl, mix together the melted margarine, 1 cup sugar, and egg until smooth. Stir in the molasses. Combine the flour, baking soda, salt, cinnamon, cloves, and ginger; blend into the molasses mixture. Cover, and chill dough for 1 hour.

Step 2

Preheat oven to 375 degrees F (190 degrees C). Roll dough into walnut sized balls, and roll them in the remaining white sugar. Place cookies 2 inches apart onto ungreased baking sheets.

Step 3

Bake for 8 to 10 minutes in the preheated oven, until tops are cracked. Cool on wire racks.

EASY LEMON COOKIES

INGREDIENTS

- 1 (18.25 ounce) package lemon cake mix
- 2 large eggs eggs
- ⅓ cup vegetable oil
- 1 teaspoon lemon extract
- ⅓ cup confectioners' sugar for decoration

DIRECTIONS

Step 1

Preheat oven to 375 degrees F (190 degrees C).

Step 2

Pour cake mix into a large bowl. Stir in eggs, oil, and lemon extract until well blended. Drop teaspoonfuls of dough into a bowl of confectioners' sugar. Roll them around until they're lightly covered. Once sugared, put them on an ungreased cookie sheet.

Step 3

Bake for 6 to 9 minutes in the preheated oven. The bottoms will be light brown, and the insides chewy.

DATE SQUARES

INGREDIENTS

- 1 ½ cups rolled oats
- 1 ½ cups sifted pastry flour
- ¼ teaspoon salt
- ¾ teaspoon baking soda
- 1 cup packed brown sugar

- ¾ cup butter, softened
- ¾ pound pitted dates, diced
- 1 cup water
- ⅓ cup packed brown sugar
- 1 teaspoon lemon juice

DIRECTIONS

Step 1

Preheat oven to 350 degrees F (175 degrees C).

Step 2

In a large bowl, combine oats, pastry flour, salt, 1 cup brown sugar, and baking soda. Mix in the butter until crumbly. Press half of the mixture into the bottom of a 9 inch square baking pan.

Step 3

In a small saucepan over medium heat, combine the dates, water, and 1/3 cup brown sugar. Bring to a boil, and cook until thickened. Stir in lemon juice, and remove from heat. Spread the filling over the base, and pat the remaining crumb mixture on top.

Step 4

Bake for 20 to 25 minutes in preheated oven, or until top is lightly toasted. Cool before cutting into squares.

THUMBPRINT COOKIES

Servings: 12 **Yield:** 2 dozen

INGREDIENTS

- ½ cup butter, softened
- ¼ cup packed brown sugar
- 1 egg
- ½ teaspoon vanilla extract
- 1 cup all-purpose flour
- ¼ cup finely chopped walnuts
- ⅔ cup any flavor fruit jam
- ¼ teaspoon salt

DIRECTIONS

Step 1

Preheat oven to 300 degrees F. Grease cookie sheets.

Step 2

Separate egg, reserving egg white. Cream butter or margarine, sugar, and egg yolk.

Step 3

Add vanilla, flour and salt, mixing well.

Step 4

Shape dough into balls. Roll in egg white, then walnuts. Place on cookie sheets about 2 inches apart. Bake for 5 minutes.

Step 5

Remove cookies from oven. With thumb, dent each cookie. Put jelly or preserves in each thumbprint. Bake for another 8 minutes.

RUM BALLS

INGREDIENTS

- 1 (12 ounce) box vanilla wafer cookies (such as Nilla)
- 1 cup semisweet chocolate chips
- ¼ cup light corn syrup
- ¾ cup dark rum (such as Meyer's)
- 1 cup confectioners' sugar, plus more for dusting

DIRECTIONS

Step 1

Place vanilla cookies in a food processor and process into fine crumbs.

Step 2

Heat chocolate chips and corn syrup together in a saucepan over low heat. Cook, stirring often, until chocolate is melted and smooth, about 5 minutes. Remove from heat and stir in rum and confectioners' sugar until smooth. Fold in cookie crumbs; dough will be sticky.

Step 3

Place saucepan in the refrigerator until dough is firm and easy to roll, about 15 minutes. Cover 2 plates with waxed paper; dust with confectioners' sugar.

Step 4

Roll dough into 1-inch balls and place on the prepared plates. Dust rum balls with confectioners' sugar. Refrigerate until firm, about 30 minutes.

Step 5

Remove rum balls from refrigerator and transfer to a resealable bag, including the extra confectioners' sugar. Seal the bag and shake to coat the rum balls completely with confectioners' sugar.

MY FAVORITE SUGAR COOKIES

INGREDIENTS

- 1 ½ cups white sugar
- ⅔ cup shortening
- 2 large eggs eggs
- 2 tablespoons milk
- 1 teaspoon vanilla extract
- 3 ¼ cups all-purpose flour
- 2 ½ teaspoons baking powder

- ½ teaspoon salt
- 1 egg white

DIRECTIONS

Step 1

Combine sugar and shortening in a mixing bowl. Beat at low speed just until smooth. Mix in eggs, milk, and vanilla.

Step 2

In separate bowl, whisk flour, baking soda and salt. Pour into sugar mixture and blend until combined.

Step 3

Shape dough into a ball and wrap with waxed paper or plastic wrap. Refrigerate 2 to 3 hours until easy to handle.

Step 4

Preheat oven to 400 degrees F (200 degrees C). Lightly grease cookie sheets or line them with parchment paper.

Step 5

Roll out half of the dough at a time on a lightly floured surface. Keep the remaining dough refrigerated. For crisp cookies, roll paper-thin. For softer cookies, roll 1/8 to 1/4 inch thick.

Step 6

With floured cookie cutters, cut dough into various shapes. Re-roll dough trimmings into a ball, cover and refrigerate, and continue to cut shapes with chilled dough.

Step 7

Place cookies 1/2 inch apart on greased cookie sheets. To glaze, brush tops of cookies with heavy or whipping cream or with an egg white slightly beaten with 1 tablespoon of water.

Step 8

Sprinkle cookies with your choice of toppings; bake 8 minutes or until very light brown. Remove cookies and cool completely.

DISH PAN COOKIES

INGREDIENTS

- 2 cups white sugar
- 2 cups light brown sugar
- 4 large eggs eggs
- 2 cups vegetable oil
- 2 teaspoons vanilla extract
- 4 cups all-purpose flour
- 2 teaspoons baking soda
- 2 teaspoons salt
- 4 cups cornflakes cereal
- 1 ½ cups rolled oats

- 1 cup flaked coconut
- 1 cup chopped pecans
- 1 cup chopped dates
- 1 cup raisins

DIRECTIONS

Step 1

Preheat oven to 325 degrees F (165 degrees C). Lightly grease a cookie sheet.

Step 2

Cream white sugar, brown sugar, eggs, vegetable oil and vanilla together in a large bowl or dishpan. In a separate bowl combine flour, baking soda and salt. Stir the flour mixture into the creamed sugar; mix until well combined.

Step 3

Stir corn flakes, oats, coconut, pecans, dates and raisins into the dough. You will most likely need to use your hands to mix everything thoroughly. Shape the dough into 1 1/2 to 2 inch balls and press them down lightly onto a greased cookie sheet.

Step 4

Bake in a preheated 325 degrees F (165 degrees C) oven for 10 to 14 minutes or until golden.

RUM OR BOURBON BALLS

INGREDIENTS

- 1 cup semisweet chocolate chips
- ½ cup white sugar
- 3 tablespoons corn syrup
- ½ cup rum
- 2 ½ cups crushed vanilla wafers
- 1 cup chopped walnuts
- ⅓ cup confectioners' sugar

DIRECTIONS

Step 1

Place chocolate chips into a microwave-safe medium bowl. Heat in the microwave for 1 minute, stir and then continue to heat at 20 second intervals, stirring between each, until melted and smooth. Stir in sugar and corn syrup. Blend in rum. Add crushed vanilla wafers and chopped nuts. Mix until evenly distributed. Cover and refrigerate until firm.

Step 2

Roll the chilled chocolate mixture into bite-size balls. Roll balls in a mixture of ground nuts and confectioner's sugar, or just plain confectioner's sugar. Store in a covered container for a week before serving to blend the flavors.

APRICOT COOKIES

Servings: 24 Yield: 4 dozen

INGREDIENTS

- 1 cup butter
- 1 cup white sugar
- 3 cups all-purpose flour
- 1 teaspoon baking powder
- ½ teaspoon salt
- 1 egg
- 1 teaspoon vanilla extract
- 1 cup apricot preserves
- ⅓ cup confectioners' sugar for decoration

DIRECTIONS

Step 1

Preheat oven to 350 degrees F (175 degrees C).

Step 2

Cream the butter and sugar in a medium size mixing bowl. Mix flour, baking powder, salt, egg and vanilla extract into the butter-sugar mixture. Cool dough in the refrigerator for 1 hour.

Step 3

On a lightly floured surface roll dough out to 1/4 inch thick. Cut the dough into rounds with a round cookie cutter or glass. Using the tip of a teaspoon place a small drop of apricot preserves into the middle of the circle. Brush edges with water and fold the dough over so that the cookie is in the shape of a half moon; seal edges Arrange on ungreased cookie sheets.

Step 4

Bake for 8 to 12 minutes, or until golden brown. Dust the cookies with powdered sugar while still hot.

Caramel Turtles Brownies

INGREDIENTS

- 1 (14 ounce) package individually wrapped caramels
- 1 (12 fluid ounce) can evaporated milk
- 1 (18.25 ounce) package chocolate cake mix
- 6 tablespoons butter, melted
- 1 cup semisweet chocolate chips
- ¼ pound whole pecans

DIRECTIONS

Step 1

Preheat oven to 350 degrees F (175 degrees C). Grease a 9x13 inch pan. Set aside.

Step 2

Unwrap caramels and place in saucepan with 2 Tablespoons evaporated milk. Melt over medium to low heat, stirring constantly.

Step 3

In a large bowl, combine the remaining evaporated milk, dry cake mix, and melted butter. Stir until well blended. Spread half of this mixture in the prepared pan. Bake for 10 minutes.

Step 4

Remove brownies from oven. Sprinkle chocolate chips and drizzle melted caramels over the top. Drop remaining cake mixture by teaspoonfuls over all. Return to oven for 20 minutes. Garnish with whole pecans if you'd like.

ALMOND CRESCENT COOKIES

INGREDIENTS

- ½ cup salted butter, at room temperature
- ⅓ cup confectioners' sugar, plus extra for dusting
- 1 teaspoon vanilla extract
- 1 teaspoon almond extract
- ⅛ teaspoon salt
- ¾ cup all-purpose flour, sifted
- 2 tablespoons all-purpose flour, sifted
- ½ cup almonds, finely chopped

DIRECTIONS

Step 1

Preheat oven to 325 degrees F (165 degrees C).

Step 2

Beat butter and confectioners' sugar in a bowl using an electric mixer until smooth and creamy. Add vanilla extract, almond extract, and salt; mix briefly to incorporate. Gradually stir 3/4 cup plus 2 tablespoons flour into the creamed butter, add almonds, and mix until dough is just combined.

Step 3

Shape dough into tiny crescents; place on an ungreased baking sheet about 2 inches apart.

Step 4

Bake cookies in preheated oven until edges are golden, about 15 minutes. Cool on the baking sheet for 5 minutes before transferring to a wire rack to cool completely.

Step 5

Roll cookies in sifted confectioners' sugar when cooled.

ANISE WALNUT BISCOTTI

INGREDIENTS

- 1 cup butter, room temperature
- 2 ½ cups white sugar

- 2 teaspoons vanilla extract
- 8 large eggs eggs
- 7 teaspoons baking powder
- 8 cups all-purpose flour
- 2 teaspoons anise extract
- 3 teaspoons anise seed
- 1 cup chopped walnuts
- 2 large egg yolks egg yolks, lightly beaten

DIRECTIONS

Step 1

Preheat oven to 375 degrees F (190 degrees C).

Step 2

In a large bowl, cream together butter and sugar Gradually add the vanilla and eggs while mixing. Sift together the flour and baking powder; stir into the egg mixture. For plain biscotti, do not add anything else (see Cook's Note). Stir in the anise extract and anise seed. Add walnuts if desired.

Step 3

Wet or grease your hands and shape dough out into 4 logs as long as your baking sheet will allow. Pat each one to about 3/4 inch in height, and 3 inches wide. Brush with beaten egg yolks.

Step 4

Bake in the preheated oven for 15 minutes, until golden brown. Slice logs at an angle, cutting pieces into 1/2 to 3/4-inch wide cookies. Place slices back onto the cookie sheet, standing upright, if possible; leave a gap between the slices. Return to the oven and bake until cookies are dry and lightly toasted, about 10 minutes more.

CHRISTMAS PINWHEEL COOKIES

INGREDIENTS

- 4 cups all-purpose flour
- 1 teaspoon baking powder
- ¼ teaspoon baking soda
- 1 teaspoon salt
- 1 ⅓ cups butter
- 1 cup packed brown sugar
- ⅔ cup white sugar
- 2 large eggs eggs, beaten
- 1 ½ teaspoons vanilla extract
- 1 drop red food coloring, or as needed
- 1 drop green food coloring, or as needed

DIRECTIONS

Step 1

Sift the flour, baking powder, baking soda, and salt together into a bowl. Resift again into another bowl.

Step 2

Beat the butter with the brown and white sugars in a mixing bowl until light and fluffy. Beat in the eggs and vanilla until smooth. Gradually stir in the flour mixture until evenly blended. Gather the dough into a ball, and divide into two equal parts. Place one half in a second bowl. Add red food coloring to the dough in one bowl, and green food coloring to the dough in the other bowl. Use a fork or wooden spoon to blend the food coloring into the dough until evenly blended. Add additional drops of food coloring to make the desired shade.

Step 3

Roll out the red dough to 1/4 inch (5mm) thickness. Roll out the green dough to 1/4 inch (5mm) thickness, and place on top of the red dough. Beginning on one edge, roll the doughs to make a log so the two colors spiral inside each other. Wrap the log in waxed paper, then in a cotton towel, and refrigerate at least 8 hours.

Step 4

Preheat oven to 400 degrees F (200 degrees C). Lightly grease 2 baking sheets.

Step 5

Unwrap the dough log, and place on a clean, lightly floured surface. Slice the log into rounds 1/8 inch (3 mm) thick, and place on prepared baking sheets.

Step 6

Bake in preheated oven until set, 5 to 6 minutes. Watch carefully to prevent edges from browning. Remove from oven, and cool on racks.

DATE TURNOVERS

INGREDIENTS

- 2 cups pitted dates, chopped
- ½ cup water
- ¼ cup brown sugar
- 1 tablespoon cider vinegar
- ½ cup milk
- 2 cups all-purpose flour
- 1 teaspoon baking soda
- 2 ½ cups regular rolled oats
- 1 ½ cups brown sugar
- ½ cup melted butter
- ½ cup butter-flavored shortening (such as Crisco), melted

DIRECTIONS

Step 1

Heat dates, water, and 1/4 cup brown sugar in a saucepan over medium heat; cook until dates are very soft, about 5 minutes. Set aside to cool to room temperature.

Step 2

Stir vinegar into milk in a bowl; set aside to curdle, about 10 minutes.

Step 3

Whisk flour and baking soda together in a large bowl; stir in oats and 1 1/2 cups brown sugar. Stir butter, shortening, and milk mixture into flour mixture; cover dough and refrigerate until firm, about 1 hour.

Step 4

Preheat oven to 350 degrees F (175 degrees C). Line baking sheets with parchment paper.

Step 5

Roll dough out on a lightly floured surface about 1/8-inch thick; cut dough circles with a round cookie cutter. Place about 1 tablespoon date mixture in the center of each circle; fold circle in half and press edges together tightly to seal. Place cookies on the prepared baking sheets.

Step 6

Bake in the preheated oven until golden, about 10 minutes. Remove to cool completely on a wire rack.

PEANUT BUTTER TEMPTATIONS

Servings: 18 **Yield:** 3 dozen

INGREDIENTS

- ½ cup butter
- ½ cup white sugar
- ½ cup packed brown sugar
- ½ cup peanut butter
- 1 egg
- ½ teaspoon vanilla extract
- 1 ¼ cups all-purpose flour
- ¾ teaspoon baking soda
- ½ teaspoon salt
- 36 eaches miniature chocolate covered peanut butter cups, unwrapped

DIRECTIONS

Step 1

Preheat oven to 375 degrees F (190 degrees C).

Step 2

In a medium bowl, cream together the brown sugar, white sugar and butter. Stir in the peanut butter, then the egg and vanilla. Sift together the flour, baking soda and salt, stir into the peanut butter mixture until the dough comes together. Shape into 1 inch balls and press them into the cups of an unprepared mini muffin pan.

Step 3

Bake for 8 to 10 minutes in the preheated oven. As soon as the cookies come out of the oven, press a mini chocolate covered peanut butter cup down into the center of each cookie until only the top is showing. Allow the cookies to cool completely before removing from their pans.

GERMAN LEBKUCHEN

INGREDIENTS

- 1 egg
- ¾ cup brown sugar
- ½ cup honey
- ½ cup dark molasses
- 3 cups sifted all-purpose flour
- ½ teaspoon baking soda
- 1 ¼ teaspoons ground nutmeg
- 1 ¼ teaspoons ground cinnamon
- ½ teaspoon ground cloves
- ½ teaspoon ground allspice
- ½ cup slivered almonds
- ½ cup candied mixed fruit peel, finely chopped
- 1 egg white, beaten
- 1 tablespoon lemon juice
- ½ teaspoon lemon zest
- 1 ½ cups sifted confectioners' sugar

DIRECTIONS

Step 1

In a large bowl, beat the egg, brown sugar and honey until smooth. Stir in the molasses. Combine the flour, baking soda, nutmeg, cinnamon, cloves and allspice; stir into the molasses mixture. Stir in the almonds and candied fruit peel. Cover or wrap dough, and chill overnight.

Step 2

Preheat the oven to 400 degrees F (200 degrees C). Grease cookie sheets. On a lightly floured surface, roll the dough out to 1/4 inch in thickness. Cut into 2x3 inch rectangles. Place cookies 1 1/2 inches apart onto cookie sheets.

Step 3

Bake for 10 to 12 minutes in the preheated oven, until firm. While still warm, brush the cookies with the lemon glaze.

Step 4

To make the glaze: In a small bowl, stir together the egg white, lemon juice and lemon zest. Mix in the confectioners' sugar until smooth. Brush over cookies.

HUNGARIAN CHESTNUT CAKE

INGREDIENTS

- ¾ pound whole chestnuts, drained
- ½ cup unsalted butter
- 4 tablespoons dark rum

- 10 (1 ounce) squares bittersweet chocolate, chopped
- 6 large eggs eggs
- ¼ teaspoon salt
- ½ cup white sugar
- 6 (1 ounce) squares bittersweet chocolate, chopped
- ½ cup heavy cream
- 1 tablespoon dark rum
- 8 eaches marrons glaces (candied chestnuts)
- 1 cup heavy cream, chilled
- 2 tablespoons white sugar
- 1 tablespoon dark rum
- ¾ cup chopped marrons glace (candied chestnuts)

DIRECTIONS

Step 1

Preheat oven to 350 degrees F (175 degrees C). Line the bottom of a greased 9-inch springform pan with parchment paper. Then grease the parchment paper.

Step 2

Separate the eggs.

Step 3

In a food processor puree the chestnuts with the butter and the rum, scraping down the sides, until the mixture is smooth. Add the melted bittersweet chocolate and blend the mixture until it is combined well. With the motor running, add the yolks, 1 at a time, and transfer the mixture to a large bowl.

Step 4

In a bowl with an electric mixer beat the whites with the salt until they hold soft peaks, add the sugar, a little at a time, beating, and beat the meringue until it holds stiff peaks.

Step 5

Whisk about one fourth of the meringue into the chocolate mixture to lighten it and fold in the remaining meringue gently but thoroughly. Pour the batter into the prepared pan and smooth the top.

Step 6

Bake the cake in the middle of a 350 degrees F (175 degrees C) oven for 45 to 55 minutes, or until a tester comes out with crumbs adhering to it and the top is cracked. Let the cake cool in the pan on a rack for 5 minutes, remove the side of the pan, and invert the cake onto another rack. Remove the bottom of the pan, invert the torte onto a rack, and let it cool completely. (The cake will fall as it cools.)

Step 7

To Make Glaze: Put 6 ounces of the finely chopped chocolate in a small bowl, in a saucepan bring 1/2 cup of the cream to a boil, and pour it over the chocolate. Stir the mixture until the chocolate is melted and the glaze is smooth and stir in 1 tablespoon of the rum. Dip each candied chestnut halfway into the glaze to coat it partially, transfer the chestnuts to a foil-covered tray, and let them set.

Step 8

Invert the cake onto a rack set on wax paper, pour the glaze over it, smoothing the glaze with a spatula and letting the excess drip down the side, and let the cake stand for 2 hours, or until the glaze is set. Transfer the cake carefully to a serving plate and garnish it with the coated chestnuts.

Step 9

Make the whipped cream just before serving the cake: In a chilled bowl with chilled beaters beat the 1 cup heavy cream until it holds soft peaks, beat in the 2 tablespoons sugar and the1 tablespoon rum, and beat the mixture until it holds stiff peaks. Fold in the chopped candied chestnuts. Serve the cake with the whipped cream.

CHOCOLATE YULE LOG

INGREDIENTS

For the Filling:

- 1 ⅔ cups powdered sugar
- ½ cup butter, at room temperature
- 1 ½ tablespoons unsweetened cocoa powder
- 1 pinch salt
- 2 tablespoons coffee-flavored liqueur
- ⅓ cup mascarpone cheese

For the Sponge Cake:

- 2 tablespoons melted butter
- ½ cup unsweetened cocoa powder
- ½ teaspoon kosher salt
- 2 tablespoons all-purpose flour
- 5 large eggs, at room temperature
- ⅔ cup white sugar
- ½ teaspoon vanilla
- 2 tablespoons powdered sugar, or as needed

For the Ganache Frosting:

- 1 cup heavy cream, boiling-hot
- 1 (8 ounce) package dark chocolate chips

DIRECTIONS

Step 1

Whip powdered sugar, butter, cocoa powder, salt, and coffee liqueur together in the bowl of a stand mixer on high speed. Transfer buttercream into a separate bowl and add mascarpone cheese. Mix until combined; set aside.

Step 2

Preheat the oven to 400 degrees F (200 degrees C). Brush a little melted butter over a 13x18-inch rimmed sheet pan. Line pan with parchment paper and brush remaining melted butter on top.

Step 3

Combine cocoa powder, salt, and flour together in a bowl; whisk or sift to break up clumps.

Step 4

Place eggs in the clean bowl of your stand mixer. Add sugar and whip until fluffy, thick, and very light in color. Add 1/2 of the cocoa powder mixture and vanilla extract; mix on low speed for a few seconds. Beat in remaining cocoa mixture on low for a few seconds. Switch to high speed; stop once mixture is moistened but not fully blended. Pull off the whisk attachment and whisk batter with it until evenly blended.

Step 5

Pour batter onto the prepared sheet pan and spread out with a spatula, leaving some room around the edges. Tap pan on the counter to knock out the large bubbles.

Step 6

Bake in the preheated oven until top is dry and edges start to pull away from the sides, 8 to 10 minutes.

Step 7

Dust a clean kitchen towel with enough powdered sugar to cover an area slightly larger than the sponge cake. Remove cake from the oven. Run a knife around the edges of the pan. Sprinkle some powdered sugar over the top. Run a spatula under the parchment paper to make sure it's not stuck to the pan.

Step 8

Quickly flip pan on top of the sugared area to invert the cake. Remove parchment paper and dust cake with more powdered sugar. Gently roll cake up inside the towel; allow to cool for 15 minutes.

Step 9

Unroll cake and dollop buttercream on top, reserving some for later. Spread frosting to the edges. Roll cake up over the frosting, using the towel to lift it if needed. Sprinkle more powdered sugar on top. Wrap log in plastic wrap. Refrigerate until firm, about 2 hours.

Step 10

Combine chocolate chips and hot cream in a bowl. Let sit for 1 minute. Whisk until chocolate melts.

Step 11

Make an angled cut 3 inches from one end of the log. Place log on a parchment-lined sheet pan. Apply some buttercream to the angled slice and attach it to one side. Spread a layer of ganache all over the cake, except for the swirls. Refrigerate for 15 minutes to firm up ganache.

Step 12

Carve lines into the ganache using the tip of a knife to create the appearance of tree bark. Refrigerate until completely chilled before serving. Dust with cocoa powder and powdered sugar.

CHEESECAKE WITH CRANBERRY GLAZE AND SUGARED CRANBERRIES

INGREDIENTS

Cheesecake:

- 10 eaches digestive biscuits (such as McVitie's)
- 5 tablespoons butter, melted

- 2 tablespoons confectioners' sugar
- ⅛ teaspoon salt
- 2 (8 ounce) packages cream cheese, softened
- ¾ cup white sugar
- 3 large eggs
- ¼ cup sour cream
- 2 teaspoons vanilla extract
- 1 orange, zested

Sugared Cranberries:

- ⅓ cup white sugar
- ½ cup water
- 1 cup fresh cranberries
- ¼ cup white sugar

Cranberry Glaze:

- 1 cup fresh cranberries
- ¼ cup water
- 2 tablespoons white sugar
- ½ cup confectioners' sugar
- 1 tablespoon orange juice
- 1 ½ teaspoons light corn syrup
- ½ teaspoon vanilla extract
- ¼ teaspoon salt

DIRECTIONS

Step 1

Preheat the oven to 375 degrees F (190 degrees C). Grease the sides of a 9-inch springform pan. Line the bottom with a circle of parchment paper.

Step 2

Crush biscuits into crumbs using a food processor. Stir crumbs, butter, confectioners' sugar, and salt together to make the crust. Press into the bottom of the pan. Rinse food processor and set aside for the cranberry glaze.

Step 3

Bake crust in the preheated oven until firm, 8 to 10 minutes. Remove the crust from the oven and reduce the temperature to 325 degrees F (165 degrees C). Let crust cool while making the filling.

Step 4

Beat cream cheese and sugar together until smooth. Add eggs, sour cream, vanilla, and orange zest. Mix until well combined, stopping to scrape the sides and bottom of the bowl. Spoon batter over the crust.

Step 5

Bake until the filling is set but still soft in the center, 30 to 40 minutes. Cool cheesecake to room temperature, about 30 minutes.

Step 6

While the cheesecake is cooling, combine 1/3 cup sugar and water in a small saucepan. Bring to a simmer over medium-low heat and stir until sugar is dissolved. Pour into a bowl and cool for 10 minutes. Add cranberries and stir to coat with syrup.

Step 7

Refrigerate cheesecake and syrup-coated cranberries, 8 hours to overnight.

Step 8

Line a rimmed baking sheet with parchment paper. Place 1/4 cup granulated sugar in a shallow bowl. Drain the cranberries, then roll them in the sugar. Place the sugared cranberries on the prepared baking sheet and allow to dry, 30 minutes to 1 hour.

Step 9

In the meantime, make the glaze. Combine cranberries, water, and sugar in a small saucepan. Simmer, crushing cranberries, until jammy, about 8 minutes. Let cool slightly. Transfer to the food processor; add confectioners' sugar, orange juice, corn syrup, vanilla, and salt. Process until smooth.

Step 10

Strain cranberry glaze through a fine-mesh sieve and discard solids. Pour over the cheesecake and smooth across the top with a small offset spatula. Garnish with sugared cranberries.

CHRISTMAS WREATH CAKE

INGREDIENTS

- 1 ½ cups raisins
- 1 cup red and green candied cherries
- ¾ cup dates, pitted and chopped
- ¾ cup candied pineapple, diced
- ¾ cup chopped walnuts
- ½ cup flaked coconut
- 3 cups all-purpose flour
- 1 teaspoon baking powder
- ½ teaspoon salt
- 1 cup butter
- 1 ¼ cups white sugar
- 1 teaspoon lemon zest
- 4 large eggs eggs
- 2 teaspoons lemon juice

DIRECTIONS

Step 1

Preheat oven to 300 degrees F (150 degrees C). Line a tube pan with 2 layers of brown paper or parchment, and grease well.

Step 2

In a large bowl, whisk together flour, baking powder, and salt. Mix in raisins, dates, cherries, pineapple, walnuts, and coconut. Stir until all fruit is coated.

Step 3

In another large bowl, cream the butter with the white sugar. Add lemon rind, lemon juice, and eggs; mix well. Stir in fruit mixture. Spread batter into prepared pan.

Step 4

Bake for 2 hours or until a tester comes out clean. Cool completely on a wire rack.

EGGNOG CHEESECAKE

INGREDIENTS

- 1 cup graham cracker crumbs
- 2 tablespoons white sugar
- 3 tablespoons melted butter
- 3 (8 ounce) packages cream cheese, softened
- 1 cup white sugar
- 3 tablespoons all-purpose flour
- ¾ cup eggnog
- 2 large eggs eggs
- 2 tablespoons rum
- 1 pinch ground nutmeg

DIRECTIONS

Step 1

Preheat oven to 325 degrees F (165 degrees C).

Step 2

In a medium bowl combine graham cracker crumbs, 2 tablespoons sugar and butter. Press into the bottom of a 9 inch spring form pan.

Step 3

Bake in preheated oven for 10 minutes. Place on a wire rack to cool.

Step 4

Preheat oven to 425 degrees F (220 degrees C).

Step 5

In a food processor combine cream cheese, 1 cup sugar, flour and eggnog; process until smooth. Blend in eggs, rum and nutmeg. Pour mixture into cooled crust.

Step 6

Bake in preheated oven for 10 minutes.

Step 7

Reduce heat to 250 and bake for 45 minutes, or until center of cake is barely firm to the touch. Remove from the oven and immediately loosen cake from rim. Let cake cool completely before removing the rim.

FAVORITE OLD FASHIONED GINGERBREAD

INGREDIENTS

- ½ cup white sugar
- ½ cup butter
- 1 egg
- 1 cup molasses
- 2 ½ cups all-purpose flour
- 1 ½ teaspoons baking soda
- 1 teaspoon ground cinnamon
- 1 teaspoon ground ginger
- ½ teaspoon ground cloves
- ½ teaspoon salt
- 1 cup hot water

DIRECTIONS

Step 1

Preheat oven to 350 degrees F (175 degrees C). Grease and flour a 9-inch square pan.

Step 2

In a large bowl, cream together the sugar and butter. Beat in the egg, and mix in the molasses.

Step 3

In a bowl, sift together the flour, baking soda, salt, cinnamon, ginger, and cloves. Blend into the creamed mixture. Stir in the hot water. Pour into the prepared pan.

Step 4

Bake 1 hour in the preheated oven, until a knife inserted in the center comes out clean. Allow to cool in pan before serving.

GLUTEN-FREE FRUITCAKE

INGREDIENTS

- ¼ cup raisins
- ¼ cup golden raisins
- ¼ cup dried cranberries
- ¼ cup dried cherries
- 5 ½ fluid ounces spiced rum
- 1 orange, zested and juiced
- ½ cup brown rice flour
- ½ cup almond meal
- ⅓ cup potato starch
- ¼ cup tapioca starch
- 1 teaspoon ground cinnamon

- ½ teaspoon ground nutmeg
- ¼ teaspoon ground cloves
- ¼ teaspoon ground cardamom
- ¼ teaspoon ground ginger
- 1 teaspoon baking powder
- 6 dates dates, pitted and chopped
- 2 figs large dried figs, chopped
- ¼ cup candied mixed fruit, chopped
- ⅔ cup butter, at room temperature
- ½ cup raw cane sugar
- 1 teaspoon vanilla extract
- 2 large eggs eggs, at room temperature
- ½ cup unsweetened applesauce
- ¼ cup whole raw hazelnuts
- ¼ cup raw walnut halves
- ¼ cup raw pecan halves
- ¼ cup raw whole almonds
- 1 ounce candied mixed fruit slices
- 3 tablespoons cherry brandy liqueur

DIRECTIONS

Step 1

Put raisins, golden raisins, cranberries, and cherries in a bowl. Pour rum and orange juice over the dried fruit. Set aside.

Step 2

Preheat the oven to 325 degrees F (165 degrees C). Butter a loaf pan.

Step 3

Whisk brown rice flour, almond meal, potato and tapioca starches, cinnamon, nutmeg, cloves, cardamom, and ginger together in a bowl. Set aside 3 tablespoons of this mixture. Add baking powder to the larger portion; mix well.

Step 4

Combine orange zest, dates, figs, and 1/4 cup candied fruit in a bowl. Sprinkle in 2 tablespoons of the reserved flour mixture and toss to coat.

Step 5

Beat butter and sugar together with an electric mixer until creamy. Mix in vanilla. Add eggs one by one, beating after each addition. Mix in applesauce.

Step 6

Drain the dried fruit, reserving the soaking liquid. Add drained fruit to the fig mixture and toss with remaining 1 tablespoon reserved flour mixture.

Step 7

Mix soaking liquid into the butter mixture. Gradually add flour, stirring just until combined; do not overmix. Fold in hazelnuts, walnut halves, and pecan halves.

Step 8

Pour batter into the prepared loaf pan. Decorate the top with almonds and candied fruit slices.

Step 9

Bake in the preheated oven for 1 hour. Reduce oven temperature to 290 degrees F (145 degrees C). Continue baking until browned on top and a toothpick inserted into the center comes out clean, about 30 minutes more.

Step 10

Remove from oven and let cool for at least 15 minutes before removing from pan. Brush cherry brandy on top. Let cake rest 24 hours for best results.

OLD-FASHIONED PERSIMMON PUDDING

INGREDIENTS

- cooking spray
- 4 cups all-purpose flour
- 1 teaspoon baking soda
- 1 teaspoon baking powder
- ½ teaspoon salt
- 1 teaspoon cinnamon
- 1 cup white sugar
- 1 cup brown sugar
- 3 large eggs eggs, beaten
- 2 cups milk
- 2 ½ cups persimmon pulp
- 6 tablespoons butter, melted

DIRECTIONS

Step 1

Preheat oven to 300 degrees F (150 degrees C). Spray a 9x13-inch baking dish with cooking spray.

Step 2

In a bowl, whisk together the flour, baking soda, baking powder, salt, cinnamon, white sugar, and brown sugar until thoroughly combined. In a large bowl, beat the eggs and milk together until smooth, and add the flour mixture, alternating with the persimmon pulp in several additions, mixing well after each addition. Stir in the melted butter. Scrape the batter into the prepared baking dish.

Step 3

Bake in the preheated oven until a toothpick inserted into the pudding comes out clean, about 1 hour. Allow to cool before serving.

BUCHE DE NOEL

INGREDIENTS

- 2 cups heavy cream
- ½ cup confectioners' sugar
- ½ cup unsweetened cocoa powder
- 1 teaspoon vanilla extract
- 6 large egg yolks egg yolks
- ½ cup white sugar
- ⅓ cup unsweetened cocoa powder
- 1 ½ teaspoons vanilla extract
- ⅛ teaspoon salt
- 6 large egg whites egg whites
- ¼ cup white sugar
- confectioners' sugar for dusting

DIRECTIONS

Step 1

Preheat oven to 375 degrees F (190 degrees C). Line a 10x15 inch jellyroll pan with parchment paper. In a large bowl, whip cream, 1/2 cup confectioners' sugar, 1/2 cup cocoa, and 1 teaspoon vanilla until thick and stiff. Refrigerate.

Step 2

In a large bowl, use an electric mixer to beat egg yolks with 1/2 cup sugar until thick and pale. Blend in 1/3 cup cocoa, 1 1/2 teaspoons vanilla, and salt. In large glass bowl, using clean beaters, whip egg whites to soft peaks. Gradually add 1/4 cup sugar, and beat until whites form stiff peaks. Immediately fold the yolk mixture into the whites. Spread the batter evenly into the prepared pan.

Step 3

Bake for 12 to 15 minutes in the preheated oven, or until the cake springs back when lightly touched. Dust a clean dishtowel with confectioners' sugar. Run a knife around the edge of the pan, and turn the warm cake out onto the towel. Remove and discard parchment paper. Starting at the short edge of the cake, roll the cake up with the towel. Cool for 30 minutes.

Step 4

Unroll the cake, and spread the filling to within 1 inch of the edge. Roll the cake up with the filling inside. Place seam side down onto a serving plate, and refrigerate until serving. Dust with confectioners' sugar before serving.

JAMAICAN FRUIT CAKE

INGREDIENTS

- 2 cups butter
- 2 cups white sugar
- 9 large eggs eggs
- ¼ cup white rum
- 1 tablespoon lime juice
- 1 teaspoon vanilla extract

- 1 tablespoon almond extract
- 1 grated zest of one lime
- 2 pounds chopped dried mixed fruit
- 2 cups red wine
- 1 cup dark molasses
- 2 ½ cups all-purpose flour
- 3 teaspoons baking powder
- ½ teaspoon ground nutmeg
- ½ teaspoon ground allspice
- ½ teaspoon ground cinnamon
- 1 pinch salt

DIRECTIONS

Step 1

Preheat oven to 350 degrees F (175 degrees C). Grease and flour 2 - 9 inch round cake pans.

Step 2

In a large bowl, cream together the butter and sugar until light and fluffy. Beat in eggs, then add rum, lime juice, vanilla, almond extract, and lime zest. Stir in mixed fruit, wine, and molasses. Sift together flour, baking powder, nutmeg, allspice, cinnamon, and salt. Fold into batter, being careful not to over-mix. Pour into prepared pans.

Step 3

Bake in preheated oven for 80 to 90 minutes, or until a knife inserted into the center comes out clean. Let cool in pan for 10 minutes, then turn out onto a wire rack and cool completely.

IRISH CREAM BUNDT CAKE

INGREDIENTS

- 1 cup chopped pecans
- 1 (18.25 ounce) package yellow cake mix
- 1 (3.4 ounce) package instant vanilla pudding mix
- 4 large eggs eggs
- ¼ cup water
- ½ cup vegetable oil
- ¾ cup Irish cream liqueur
- ½ cup butter
- ¼ cup water
- 1 cup white sugar
- ¼ cup Irish cream liqueur

DIRECTIONS

Step 1

Preheat oven to 325 degrees F (165 degrees C). Grease and flour a 10 inch Bundt pan. Sprinkle chopped nuts evenly over bottom of pan.

Step 2

In a large bowl, combine cake mix and pudding mix. Mix in eggs, 1/4 cup water, 1/2 cup oil and 3/4 cup Irish cream liqueur. Beat for 5 minutes at high speed. Pour batter over nuts in pan.

Step 3

Bake in the preheated oven for 60 minutes, or until a toothpick inserted into the cake comes out clean. Cool for 10 minutes in the pan, then invert onto the serving dish. Prick top and sides of cake. Spoon glaze over top and brush onto sides of cake. Allow to absorb glaze repeat until all glaze is used up.

Step 4

To make the glaze: In a saucepan, combine butter, 1/4 cup water and 1 cup sugar. Bring to a boil and continue boiling for 5 minutes, stirring constantly. Remove from heat and stir in 1/4 cup Irish cream.

CREAMY COCONUT CAKE

INGREDIENTS

- 1 (16 ounce) package white cake mix
- 1 (14 ounce) can cream of coconut
- 1 (14 ounce) can sweetened condensed milk
- 1 (16 ounce) container frozen whipped topping, thawed
- 1 (10 ounce) package flaked coconut

DIRECTIONS

Step 1

Prepare cake according to package directions. Bake in a 9x13 inch pan. Cool completely.

Step 2

In a small bowl combine cream of coconut and condensed milk.

Step 3

Poke holes in cake with a straw. Pour milk mixture over cake and spread with whipped topping. Sprinkle coconut over cake.

Step 4

Serve chilled.

FIGGY PUDDING

INGREDIENTS

- 1 ¾ cups buttermilk
- 12 ounces dried Calimyrna figs, coarsely chopped
- 1 ½ cups white whole-wheat flour (such as King Arthur)
- 1 cup white sugar
- 2 ½ teaspoons baking powder
- 1 teaspoon ground nutmeg
- 1 teaspoon ground cinnamon
- 1 teaspoon salt

- 3 eaches eggs
- 1 ½ cups dry bread crumbs
- ½ cup butter, melted
- 1 (2.45 ounce) package sliced almonds
- 3 tablespoons orange marmalade
- 1 tablespoon grated orange zest
- ½ teaspoon orange-vanilla flavoring (such as Fiori di Sicilia

DIRECTIONS

Step 1

Gently heat buttermilk and figs in a saucepan over medium-low heat until softened, 10 to 15 minutes; set aside until cool.

Step 2

Preheat oven to 350 degrees F (175 degrees C). Grease a tube pan.

Step 3

Sift flour, sugar, baking powder, nutmeg, cinnamon, and salt together in a bowl.

Step 4

Beat eggs in a large bowl with an electric hand mixer on high for 1 minute. Add fig-and-buttermilk mixture, bread crumbs, butter, almonds, orange marmalade, orange zest, and orange-vanilla flavoring to the beaten eggs; beat on low speed until blended. Gradually add flour mixture while beating until just incorporated into a batter. Spoon batter into prepared pan. Grease a sheet of aluminum foil; use to cover pan.

Step 5

Bake in preheated oven until firm and pulling away from sides of the pan, about 2 hours. Set aside to cool for 10 minutes before removing from pan.

PUMPKIN SWIRLED CHEESE CAKE

INGREDIENTS

- 1 ½ cups crushed shortbread cookies
- 3 tablespoons melted butter
- 3 tablespoons unbleached all-purpose flour
- ¾ cup white sugar
- ¼ cup brown sugar
- 3 tablespoons unbleached all-purpose flour
- 1 (8 ounce) package cream cheese, softened
- 1 (3 ounce) package cream cheese, softened
- 1 tablespoon vanilla extract
- 1 teaspoon ground cinnamon
- ¼ teaspoon ground nutmeg
- ¼ teaspoon ground ginger
- 3 large eggs eggs
- 1 (15 ounce) can pumpkin puree

- 1 tablespoon milk

DIRECTIONS

Step 1

Preheat oven to 375 degrees F (190 degrees C.)

Step 2

In a medium bowl, mix crushed cookies, 3 tablespoons melted butter and 3 tablespoons flour. Press firmly on bottom and side of ungreased 9 inch pie plate. Bake about 12 minutes or until light brown. Allow to cool.

Step 3

In a large bowl, combine white sugar, brown sugar, flour, and cream cheese. Beat on low speed until smooth. Reserve 1/2 cup of this mixture to swirl in later. To the mixture in the bowl, add vanilla, cinnamon, nutmeg, ginger. Blend in eggs and pumpkin puree. Scrape bowl, and beat until smooth. Pour into crust.

Step 4

Stir 1 tablespoon milk into the reserved cream cheese mixture. Drop by spoonfuls over the pumpkin mixture. Use a knife to decoratively swirl the two mixtures together.

Step 5

Cover edge of crust with 2 to 3 inch strip of aluminum foil to prevent excessive browning. Bake in preheated 35 to 40 minutes or until knife inserted in center comes out clean. Remove foil the last 15 minutes of baking. Cool 30 minutes, then refrigerate at least 4 hours before serving.

TENNESSEE JAM CAKE

INGREDIENTS

- 1 cup butter, softened
- 2 cups white sugar
- 8 large eggs eggs
- 2 teaspoons baking soda
- 2 tablespoons water
- 2 cups seedless blackberry jam
- 3 ½ cups all-purpose flour
- 1 ½ teaspoons ground cloves
- 2 teaspoons ground nutmeg
- 1 tablespoon ground cinnamon
- 1 teaspoon salt
- 1 cup buttermilk
- 1 cup chopped black walnuts
- ½ cup golden raisins

DIRECTIONS

Step 1

Preheat the oven to 350 degrees F (175 degrees C). Grease three 8 or 9 inch round cake pans and set aside.

Step 2

In a large bowl, beat butter and sugar until light and fluffy. Add eggs one at a time, mixing until each one is blended in. Dissolve the baking soda in the water; stir into the batter along with the blackberry jam. Combine the flour, cloves, nutmeg, cinnamon and salt; stir into the batter by hand, alternating with the buttermilk. Fold in the black walnuts and raisins if using. Divide the batter equally between the three pans, and spread in an even layer.

Step 3

Bake in the preheated oven until the top of the cakes spring back when lightly touched, about 35 minutes. Cool in the pans until cool enough to handle, then invert the cakes over a wire rack and remove pans to cool completely.

ULTIMATE CRANBERRY PUDDING CAKE

INGREDIENTS

- 6 tablespoons butter
- 2 cups white sugar
- 4 cups all-purpose flour
- 4 teaspoons baking powder
- 1 teaspoon salt
- 2 cups evaporated milk
- 1 (12 ounce) package cranberries
- 1 cup butter
- 2 cups white sugar
- 1 cup heavy cream
- 1 teaspoon vanilla extract

DIRECTIONS

Step 1

Preheat oven to 325 degrees F (165 degrees C). Grease and flour a 10 inch Bundt pan. Mix together the flour, baking powder and salt. Set aside.

Step 2

In a large bowl, cream together the 6 tablespoons butter and 2 cups sugar until light and fluffy. Beat in the flour mixture alternately with the evaporated milk. Stir in the cranberries. Pour batter into prepared pan.

Step 3

Bake in the preheated oven for 50 to 60 minutes, or until a toothpick inserted into the center of the cake comes out clean. Let cool in pan for 10 minutes, then turn out onto a wire rack and cool completely.

Step 4

To make the Hot Butter Sauce: In a saucepan, combine 1 cup butter, 2 cups sugar, and cream. Bring to a boil over medium heat, reduce heat and let simmer for 10 minutes. Remove from heat and stir in vanilla. Serve slices of cake generously covered with hot butter sauce.

IRISH CREAM CHEESECAKE

INGREDIENTS

- 1 cup graham cracker crumbs
- 3 tablespoons white sugar
- 3 tablespoons melted butter
- 3 (8 ounce) packages cream cheese
- 1 cup white sugar
- 2 teaspoons vanilla extract
- 1 cup sour cream
- ⅓ cup Irish cream liqueur
- 4 large eggs eggs
- 1 cup sour cream
- ¼ cup white sugar

DIRECTIONS

Step 1

Mix together cracker crumbs, 3 tablespoons sugar, and melted butter. Press this crumb mixture into bottom of 9 inch springform pan with 2 3/4 inch high sides. Bake at 350 degrees F (175 degrees) until brown - about 8 minutes. Transfer crust to rack and cool. Maintain oven temperature.

Step 2

Using electric mixer, beat cream cheese, 1 cup sugar and vanilla in large bowl until blended. Beat in 1 cup sour cream and liqueur. Add eggs one at a time, beating just until combined. Pour filling over crust in pan. Bake until edges are puffed, and center no longer moves when pan is shaken, about 1 to 1/2 hours. Transfer cheesecake to rack, and cool 10 minutes. Maintain oven temperature.

Step 3

Mix 1 cup sour cream and 1/4 cup sugar in a small bowl until smooth. Press down edges of cheesecake, and spread mixture on top. Bake 10 minutes. Transfer cheesecake to rack and cool. Cover and refrigerate overnight. Release pan from cheesecake. Cut and serve.

MARITIME WAR CAKE

INGREDIENTS

- 2 cups water
- 2 cups raisins
- 1 cup light molasses
- 1 cup white sugar
- ⅔ cup shortening
- 3 cups all-purpose flour
- 1 teaspoon baking soda

- 1 tablespoon ground cinnamon

DIRECTIONS

Step 1

Preheat oven to 325 degrees F (165 degrees C). Grease and flour a round tube pan or two loaf pans.

Step 2

Bring water, raisins, molasses, sugar, and shortening to a boil in a saucepan; reduce heat to low and simmer until raisins are plump, about 5 minutes. Allow to cool.

Step 3

Whisk flour, baking soda, and cinnamon together in a bowl. Stir flour mixture into raisin mixture until well combined; pour into prepared baking pan.

Step 4

Bake in the preheated oven until a toothpick inserted near the center comes out clean, about 1 hour.

PLUM BREAD

INGREDIENTS

- 1 cup vegetable oil
- 3 large eggs eggs
- 2 (4 ounce) jars plum baby food
- 2 cups white sugar
- 1 teaspoon red food coloring
- 2 cups all-purpose flour
- 1 teaspoon ground cloves
- 1 teaspoon ground cinnamon
- ½ teaspoon ground nutmeg
- ½ teaspoon salt
- ½ teaspoon baking soda
- 1 cup chopped nuts
- 1 cup confectioners' sugar
- 2 ½ tablespoons lemon juice

DIRECTIONS

Step 1

Preheat oven to 350 degrees F (175 degrees C). Grease and flour a bundt pan or loaf pans.

Step 2

In a large bowl, mix together vegetable oil, white sugar, eggs, plum baby food, and food coloring. In a separate bowl, mix together flour, cloves, cinnamon, nutmeg, salt, baking soda, and nuts.

Step 3

Mix wet and dry ingredients together. Transfer batter to prepared pan(s).

Step 4

Bake in the preheated oven for 50-60 minutes or until a tester comes out clean. (Smaller loaf pans will take less time.)

Step 5

Remove from oven to cool 10 minutes in pan. Remove and place on cooling rack.

Step 6

While the cake is cooling, combine confectioners' sugar and lemon juice. Brush over top while cake is still hot.

POPCORN CAKE

INGREDIENTS

- 4 quarts popped popcorn
- 1 pound candy-coated chocolate pieces
- 1 cup peanuts
- ⅓ cup vegetable oil
- ½ cup butter
- 1 pound marshmallows

DIRECTIONS

Step 1

Mix popcorn, M&Ms, and peanuts in large bowl.

Step 2

Heat oil, butter, and marshmallows in pan until melted. Pour over popcorn and blend together with heavy spoon or hands.

Step 3

Spray Bundt cake pan with vegetable spray. Press mixture lightly into pan and refrigerate until cool.

Step 4

To remove cake from pan, put pan in warm water, then turn upside down until cake comes out.

GINGERBREAD CUPCAKES

INGREDIENTS

- 1 (18.25 ounce) box vanilla cake mix
- ½ cup buttermilk
- ½ cup molasses
- ⅓ cup vegetable oil
- 4 large eggs large eggs
- 1 ½ teaspoons ground ginger
- ½ teaspoon ground cinnamon
- ¼ teaspoon ground nutmeg

DIRECTIONS

Step 1

Preheat oven to 350 degrees F (175 degrees C). Line 24 muffin cups with paper muffin liners.

Step 2

Mix the cake mix, buttermilk, molasses, vegetable oil, eggs, ginger, cinnamon, and nutmeg together in large bowl until just combined. Spoon the batter into a large resealable plastic bag, press out excess air, and seal the top of the bag. Snip a corner of the bag about 1/4-inch from the bottom. Pipe the batter into the prepared muffin cups, filling them about 2/3 full.

Step 3

Bake in the preheated oven until a toothpick inserted into the center comes out clean, 15 to 20 minutes. Cool in the pans for 10 minutes before removing to cool completely on a wire rack.

EASY RED VELVET CAKE

INGREDIENTS

- 1 (18.25 ounce) package white cake mix
- 1 (3.5 ounce) package non-instant chocolate pudding mix
- red food coloring, as desired
- ½ cup buttermilk

DIRECTIONS

Step 1

Preheat oven to 350 degrees F (175 degrees C).

Step 2

Prepare cake according to package directions, substituting half of the water called for with buttermilk (approximately 1/2 cup). Stir in pudding mix and food coloring.

Step 3

Pour into cake pan(s) and bake according to package directions.

PLUM PUDDING

INGREDIENTS

- ¼ cup butter
- ⅓ cup brown sugar
- 1 cup milk
- 12 dates dates, pitted and chopped
- ½ cup raisins
- ¼ cup dried currants
- ¼ cup candied mixed fruit peel, chopped
- 1 orange, zested
- 1 teaspoon baking soda
- 1 cup self-rising flour
- 2 teaspoons ground cinnamon
- 1 pinch salt

DIRECTIONS

Step 1

Well grease a pudding mold.

Step 2

In a large saucepan combine butter, sugar, milk, dates, raisins, currants, mixed fruit peel and zest of the orange; bring to a boil. Remove from heat and stir in baking soda. Sift in the flour, cinnamon and salt; mix gently until blended. Pour into prepared pudding mold.

Step 3

Cover with a double layer of greased wax paper and steam for 2 hours.

WALNUT-CREAM ROLL

INGREDIENTS

- 4 large egg whites egg whites
- 1 teaspoon vanilla extract
- ½ teaspoon salt
- ½ cup white sugar
- 4 large egg yolks egg yolks
- ¼ cup sifted enriched flour
- ½ cup chopped walnuts
- 1 tablespoon sifted confectioners' sugar, or as needed
- 1 cup cold heavy cream
- 1 tablespoon white sugar, or to taste
- 1 tablespoon walnut halves, or as needed

DIRECTIONS

Step 1

Preheat the oven to 375 degrees F (190 degrees C). Line the bottom and sides of a 15 1/2x10 1/2x1-inch jelly roll pan with waxed paper.

Step 2

Beat egg whites, vanilla extract, and salt using an electric mixer in a mixing bowl until soft peaks form. Beat in 1/2 cup white sugar gradually until combined.

Step 3

Beat egg yolks in a separate bowl using an electric mixer until thick and lemon-colored. Fold into egg white mixture. Fold in flour and chopped walnuts carefully until combined. Spread batter into the prepared jelly roll pan.

Step 4

Bake in the preheated oven until cake springs back when lightly touched and a toothpick inserted into the center comes out clean, about 12 minutes.

Step 5

Remove from the oven and let cool for 5 minutes. Loosen sides of cake; turn out onto a towel sprinkled with sifted confectioners' sugar. Peel off wax paper and let cool to lukewarm, 5 to 10 minutes.

Step 6

Roll cake and towel together starting at the narrow end. Let cool completely on a wire rack, 15 to 20 minutes.

Step 7

While cake cools, beat cold heavy cream and 1 tablespoon white sugar together in a mixing bowl using an electric mixer just until stiff peaks form.

Step 8

Unroll cake and spread with whipped cream, reserving some for topping. Re-roll cake and let chill in the refrigerator for at least 30 minutes. Top with dollops of whipped cream and walnut halves. Slice and serve.

BEST PUMPKIN CHEESECAKE

INGREDIENTS

- 3 (8 ounce) packages cream cheese
- 1 cup white sugar
- 1 cup sour cream
- 1 teaspoon vanilla extract
- 1 tablespoon pumpkin pie spice
- 6 large eggs eggs
- 1 cup pumpkin puree
- 2 (9 inch) prepared graham cracker crusts

DIRECTIONS

Step 1

Preheat oven to 375 degrees F (190 degrees C.)

Step 2

In a large bowl, beat cream cheese and sugar until smooth. Blend in sour cream, vanilla and spice. Beat in eggs, one at a time. Blend in pumpkin puree until no streaks remain. Pour filling into 2 crusts.

Step 3

Bake in the preheated oven for 45 minutes, or until filling is set. Allow to cool, then refrigerate at least 4 hours before serving.

LEMON SUNSHINE CAKE

INGREDIENTS

- 1 (18.25 ounce) package lemon cake mix
- 1 (3 ounce) package instant lemon pudding mix
- ½ cup white sugar
- 4 large eggs eggs
- 1 cup peach nectar

- ½ cup vegetable oil
- 2 cups sifted confectioners' sugar
- ¼ cup peach nectar
- 1 tablespoon lemon juice
- 1 teaspoon grated lemon peel

DIRECTIONS

Step 1

Preheat oven to 350 degrees F (175 degrees C).

Step 2

Grease and flour a 10-inch fluted tube pan (such as a Bundt).

Step 3

Beat lemon cake mix, lemon pudding mix, white sugar, eggs, 1 cup peach nectar, and vegetable oil in a bowl with electric mixer on medium speed for 2 minutes.

Step 4

Pour batter into prepared cake pan.

Step 5

Bake in preheated oven until top of cake springs back when lightly pressed and a toothpick inserted into the middle of the cake comes out clean, about 50 minutes.

Step 6

Cool cake in the pan for 15 minutes before removing cake to finish cooling on rack.

Step 7

Mix confectioners' sugar, 1/4 cup peach nectar, lemon juice, and lemon peel in a bowl to make a smooth frosting.

Step 8

Place cake on a serving platter; poke holes in top of the cake with a fork. Pour frosting slowly over the cake, allowing frosting to soak into the holes and drizzle down the sides of the cake.

GRANDMA'S SUET PUDDING

INGREDIENTS

- 1 cup milk
- 1 teaspoon lemon juice
- 1 cup chopped suet
- 1 cup molasses
- 1 teaspoon baking soda
- 2 cups all-purpose flour
- 1 cup raisins
- 1 egg white, beaten
- 9 tablespoons confectioners' sugar

- vanilla extract to taste

DIRECTIONS

Step 1

Sour the milk by adding the lemon juice.

Step 2

In a large bowl combine suet, molasses, soured milk, baking soda, flour and raisins. Place batter in a pudding mold or large double boiler and steam, uncovered, for 2 hours.

Step 3

To make the sauce combine, in a small saucepan, the egg white, confectioner's sugar and vanilla. Heat over medium until thickened. Serve over warm pudding.

GRANDMA'S FRUIT CAKE

INGREDIENTS

- 3 cups water
- 1 ½ cups raisins
- 3 cups all-purpose flour
- 2 tablespoons ground cinnamon
- 1 ½ tablespoons baking powder
- 1 tablespoon baking soda
- ½ teaspoon salt
- 1 pound pecan halves
- 2 tablespoons all-purpose flour
- 2 cups white sugar
- 1 ½ cups canola oil
- 4 large eggs eggs, beaten
- 3 cups candied fruit

DIRECTIONS

Step 1

Preheat oven to 350 degrees F (175 degrees C). Grease two 8x8-inch baking pans.

Step 2

Bring water and raisins to a boil in a saucepan; cook until raisins are plump, about 2 minutes. Drain and cool raisins; reserve raisin water.

Step 3

Mix 3 cups flour, cinnamon, baking powder, baking soda, and salt together in a bowl. Place pecans and 2 tablespoons flour in a resealable plastic bag; close and shake bag until pecans are coated. Pour pecans into a colander and shake off excess flour.

Step 4

Whisk sugar, oil, eggs, and cooled raisin water together in a bowl; fold in candied fruit. Stir flour mixture, 1/2 cup at a time, into sugar mixture until fully incorporated; fold in raisins and pecans. Fill the prepared pans a little over half full.

Step 5

Bake in the preheated oven for 40 minutes. Lower temperature to 325 degrees F (165 degrees C); bake until a knife inserted in the center of the cake comes out clean, about 1 more hour.

DUNDEE CAKE

Servings: 12 **Yield:** 1 cake

INGREDIENTS

- 1 cup raisins
- 1 cup dried currants
- ⅓ cup diced candies mixed fruit peel
- ⅓ cup candied cherries, quartered
- 2 tablespoons grated orange zest
- ⅓ cup all-purpose flour
- 1 cup butter, softened
- 1 cup white sugar
- 4 large eggs eggs
- 1 ⅔ cups all-purpose flour
- 1 teaspoon baking powder
- 1 ounce ground almonds
- ½ cup whole almonds
- 1 tablespoon corn syrup

DIRECTIONS

Step 1

Combine raisins, currants, mixed peel, cherries, and orange rind. Dredge with 1/3 cup flour.

Step 2

Cream butter or margarine and sugar until fluffy. Beat in eggs 1 at a time until light. Combine 1 2/3 cups flour, baking powder, and ground almonds; fold into batter mixture. Mix in fruit. Spread in foil lined 8 x 3 inch round pan. If using a different size pan fill 3/4 full.

Step 3

Bake at 325 degrees F (165 degrees C) for about 1 1/2 hours, until an inserted wooden pick comes out clean. Remove cake from pan.

Step 4

Toast almonds in 350 degrees F (175 degrees C) oven until lightly browned, about 5 minutes. Heat corn syrup, and brush over top surface of hot cake. Place almonds in whatever design you like. After cooling, cake will not be sticky.

BEST EVER NEW ZEALAND PAVLOVA

INGREDIENTS

- 3 large egg whites egg whites

- 1 ¼ cups white sugar
- 2 tablespoons water
- 3 teaspoons cornstarch
- ½ teaspoon vanilla extract
- 1 teaspoon distilled white vinegar
- ⅛ teaspoon salt

DIRECTIONS

Step 1

Preheat oven to 275 degrees F (135 degrees C). Grease a cookie sheet, line it with parchment paper and sprinkle a little water over paper.

Step 2

In a large glass or metal mixing bowl, beat egg whites until foamy. Gradually add sugar, continuing to beat until stiff peaks form. Beat in water, then mix in cornstarch, vanilla, vinegar and salt.

Step 3

Pour entire meringue mixture onto the center of the pan. Pavlova will spread as it bakes.

Step 4

Bake in the preheated oven for 45 minutes. Turn oven off and leave Pavlova in the oven until cold. Turn upside-down onto plate and top with fresh fruit and whipped cream.

STREUSEL COFFEE CAKE

INGREDIENTS

- 1 cup butter
- 2 cups white sugar
- 4 large eggs eggs
- 2 cups sour cream
- 2 teaspoons vanilla extract
- 4 cups all-purpose flour
- 2 teaspoons baking powder
- 2 teaspoons baking soda
- ½ cup white sugar
- 2 teaspoons ground cinnamon
- 1 cup chopped walnuts

DIRECTIONS

Step 1

Preheat oven to 350 degrees F (175 degrees C). Grease and flour a 10 inch Bundt pan. In a medium bowl, mix the flour, baking powder and baking soda together and set aside. In a separate small bowl, combine 1/2 cup sugar, cinnamon, and nuts. Set aside.

Step 2

In a large bowl, cream butter and 2 cups white sugar until light and fluffy. Add eggs, sour cream, and vanilla extract. Add flour mixture and beat until well combined.

Step 3

Pour half of batter into Bundt pan. Sprinkle half of the nut mixture on top of batter in pan. Add remaining batter, and sprinkle with the last of the nut mixture.

Step 4

Bake at 350 degrees F (175 degrees C) for 45 to 60 minutes, or until a toothpick inserted into cake comes out clean.